Levi Barbour

B. Creek

THE AMERICAN DEBATER.

Dan'l Webster

THE

AMERICAN DEBATER:

BEING

A PLAIN EXPOSITION OF THE PRINCIPLES AND PRACTICE OF PUBLIC DEBATE:

WHEREIN WILL BE FOUND,

AN ACCOUNT OF THE QUALIFICATIONS NECESSARY TO A GOOD DELIBERATIVE ORATOR, AS ALSO THE MODE OF ACQUIRING THEM, THE RULES OF ORDER OBSERVED IN DELIBERATIVE ASSEMBLIES, DEBATES IN FULL, AND IN OUTLINE, ON VARIOUS INTERESTING TOPICS, NUMEROUS QUESTIONS FOR DISCUSSION, FORMS OF A CONSTITUTION FOR LITERARY CLUBS OR DEBATING SOCIETIES, ETC., ETC.

BY JAMES N. McELLIGOTT, LL.D.,

AUTHOR OF "THE ANALYTICAL MANUAL," "YOUNG ANALYZER," ETC

"Here is a thing wherein I would willingly have you agree, that is, to DISPUTE and not to QUARREL; for friends *dispute* between themselves for their better instruction, and enemies *quarrel* to destroy one another."—PLATO.

NEW YORK:
IVISON & PHINNEY, 178 FULTON STREET;
(SUCCESSORS OF NEWMAN & IVISON, AND MARK H. NEWMAN & CO.)
CHICAGO: S. C. GRIGGS & CO., 111 LAKE STREET.
BUFFALO: PHINNEY & CO., 188 MAIN STREET
CINCINNATI: MOORE, WILSTACH, KEYS & CO.
AUBURN: SEYMOUR & CO.

1855.

STEREOTYPED BY
THOMAS B. SMITH,
84 Beekman St. N. Y.

PRINTED BY
J. D. TORREY,
18 Spruce Street.

CONTENTS.

SECTION VIII.

SECTION IX.

SECTION X.

SECTION XI.

SECTION XII.

SECTION XIII.

SECTION XIV.

APPENDIX.

PREFACE.

THE aim of this work is not *novelty*, but *utility*. Its merit, therefore, if any it has, consists not in the development of new ideas and principles, but rather in working into shape, convenient for reference and for teaching, materials which, in some form or other, every one should have, who aspires to be a good debater.

That the youth of our country ought to be conversant with the principles and practice of public debate, that is, ought to be instructed in the arts of speaking and in the modes of proceeding proper to a deliberative assembly, will immediately appear, if we but consider the important interests, social, civil and religious, which often hang upon the decisions of bodies of this nature. The time has come, when public speaking, not that alone which is the result of careful premeditation, but that, especially, which, in order to defend truth in the moment of her danger, must itself be the offspring of the moment, can be no otherwise considered than as a necessary preparation for the active duties of life.

To those, therefore, who feel the force of this sentiment, to all, in short, who, for any cause, deem it wise to fit and furnish themselves for effective service in public discussion, this volume is offered; not as exhausting the subject, or introducing everything that might be desired in the case, but as affording important, if not essential, *aid.*

To those instructors who hold, with the author, that debates, oral or written, or both, are quite legitimate scholastic exercises, and better calculated than most other exercises in speaking and writing, to awaken interest and secure proficiency, this work is commended as a suitable text-book, wherewith the subject may be brought up in regular recitations, and the precepts inculcated immediately reduced to practice.

To those, finally, who have passed the precincts of youth, and have had, or are anxious to have, some practical skill in doing what is requisite to be done in deliberative assemblies, the author ventures to tender the following pages, as containing such hints, and suggestions, and instructions, respecting the qualifications of a good debater, and the rules of order in the transaction of business, as may render it, perchance, a valuable book of reference.

Such is the design of the present publication. Its plan, which may be discovered at a glance, is perfectly simple; for it aspires to no higher office than that of being a plain, though reliable guide in the matters, whereof it undertakes to speak.

SECTION I.

INTRODUCTORY OBSERVATIONS.

THE endowments, both natural and acquired, essential to the formation of a finished debater, are rare and various. Few, accordingly, ever reach the highest distinction in deliberative oratory.

But, by reasonable study and practice, every person of ordinary ability may easily acquire such skill in debating, as will enable him to acquit himself decently, if not handsomely, in a public assembly. This being the case, it becomes the interest, because it is the duty, of every American youth to prepare himself, as best he can, to figure advantageously in deliberative bodies.

In so doing, however, some guidance seems necessary; for, as he that travels, in foreign lands, without a guide, is apt to travel to very little purpose, so he that labors to become a good debater, without suitable direction, is most likely to miss the aim of his best endeavors. He ought, at least, definitely to ascertain what defects he is to cure, what errors he should avoid.

To give this information, to be, in short, a sort of friendly guide to the principles and practice of debating in public, the following pages are designed. They assume that the young debater ought to know what is peculiar to the line of speaking, in which he wishes to excel, and that in order to understand *that*, one way (among many) is to consider the relations which it sustains to the several other great branches of public eloquence.

Accordingly, the question is raised,—"*What is a good debater?*" and, by way of answer, the special province of deliberative eloquence is carefully marked out, and the chief qualifications for an able deliberative orator given in detail.

But, as among the qualifications set down as necessary to success in debating, extemporaneous speaking is particularly specified, because it is of the highest importance, the section next in order is devoted exclusively to that subject.

The young debater may, however, be seriously embarrassed by a want of acquaintance with those rules of order which are in general use in deliberative assemblies. Hence, a large portion of the work is occupied with a course of instruction, in the form of question and answer, designed to render him familiar with what is aptly called *the common code of Parliamentary law.*

But, when well provided in all other respects, there is a particular duty implied and involved in the very act of undertaking publicly to discuss a question, in the performance of which some aid or advice may be necessary. That duty is to study how best to treat the question; and, therefore, under the caption, "*Management of a Question,*" the student will find some directions that may prove both timely and serviceable.

To gratify those who might expect to find in the book the form of a debate in full, two questions have been proposed and formally discussed. This has been done, moreover, under the impression that some idea of the modes of attack and defense, usual in debate, some notion of the *modus operandi* in general, might be better conveyed in this way than in any other.

The full debates are followed by a series of skeleton or outline debates; that is, questions with a summary of arguments, or rather considerations on both sides, designed merely to intimate certain lines of thought, that may be varied and extended by the reader's own reflections.

Next, in order, follows a series of questions, with references, under each, to authorities or sources of information on the matters, concerning which they challenge dispute.

After these, is inserted an extensive list of debatable questions, in respect to which the reader is left to act as an independent reasoner: thinking and consulting as his judgment and intelligence may direct.

To serve the convenience of those who may, perhaps, for the first time, be appointed to draft Rules and Regulations for a Debating or Literary Society, the last Section of the work is devoted to the presentation of two different forms of a Constitution and By-Laws, suitable for such an association.

SECTION II.

WHAT IS A GOOD DEBATER?

TO estimate the importance of being a good debater, or ascertain the qualifications essential to that character, it is necessary briefly to consider the aim and scope of deliberative eloquence.

All public speaking, except that of the pulpit,* considered in reference to its *aim*, falls under one or other of these three ancient divisions,—Demonstrative,† Judicial, or Deliberative.

The demonstrative has its place where great events or great persons are to be celebrated. It employs, upon occasion, the language of invective, but its particular province is elaborate eulogy. Its appropriate times are the memorable anniversaries, the days of great public solemnity, the extraordinary occasions,

* Pulpit eloquence is here excepted, because it does not properly fall under any one of these three heads, but, in reality, embraces the leading features of them all.

† The term *demonstrative* (from the Latin *demonstro, to show or point out clearly*), is here used, as among the Latin rhetoricians, to signify what is *showy*, or *abounding in show or ornament*, i. e. *laudatory, glorifying.*

whatever their name or their nature, whereon men meet to mingle and express their common sympathies. It is expected to display the riches of rhetoric, and to exert every force and every fascination of oratory. Its strong appeal is to the heart. Its purpose is the praise of virtue or the reprobation of vice.

The judicial is that which is engaged in the litigation of causes, in the adjustment of disputed rights, in the determination of guilt or innocence. Its scene is the court-house. It is, in style, clear, direct, and logical. It deals in law and evidence, sifts and weighs testimony, and labors every way to convince the understanding. In short, its appeal is to the head, its aim the administration of justice.

The deliberative is that which is employed where propositions, after being duly discussed, are finally to be adopted or rejected, according to the pleasure of the assembly. It differs from the demonstrative and the judicial, both in the end which it seeks, and the means which it employs for the attainment of that end.

The demonstrative, as before intimated, begins and ends in display. It abounds in ornament; it awakens emotion; it delights the imagination; it exhibits the virtues of its subject, but no less exhibits the resources of rhetoric and the talents of the orator. But here its mission closes. It looks to no definite resulting action in the body addressed.

The judicial, unlike the demonstrative, avoids every appearance of show, or endeavor. It relies upon facts, evidence, positive statute; counts little upon appeals to the emotional nature; but demands a verdict, not as a favor, but as a right, not as being expedient, but as being nothing more than what is just.

The deliberative differs from the demonstrative, in laboring to sway the opinions of the audience, and to secure a vote in favor of what it claims to be best. It differs from the judicial, in recognizing in the body addressed a perfect freedom of choice. The demonstrative deals with our affections; the judicial appeals to our judgment of right and wrong; the deliberative calls for the exercise of wisdom in relation to what is useful, what is expedient, what is best to be done.

The occasions for the use of deliberative eloquence are now more numerous and important than they ever have been in any previous age of the world. Wherever the will of the people is the law of the land, wherever republican principles prevail to any considerable extent, there deliberative assemblies must often be convened.

In our own country, accordingly, they abound in every quarter, and consider every topic of common interest. The Congress of the United States is a deliberative assembly. The Legislatures of the several States are deliberative assemblies. Every town meeting, every county gathering, every State or National Convention, every association of persons, whatever the purposes of the association, constitutes a deliberative assembly. In all these, propositions are submitted for consideration, discussed with freedom, and received, or rejected, according to the will of the body.

The variety of interests involved in the transactions of bodies of this nature, and the necessity of preventing party sway and hasty action, render it important for every one to be ready to exert a wholesome influence in their deliberations. Few men, comparatively, ever have opportunity or inclination to exercise their talents in the composition and delivery of set orations or lectures adapted to particular times and occasions. But to speak in a deliberative assembly, to enlighten and sway the minds of men engaged in the consideration of momentous affairs, may be the lot of every one. Hence, every man owes it to the community in which he lives, no less than to his own honor and interest, to fit himself, as far as may be, to discharge this most important duty.

From this brief survey of the nature and extent of deliberative eloquence, may easily be inferred the qualifications proper to be sought by him who aspires to the character of a good debater.

In certain general qualities he must, of course, share with the orator in every other field of oratory. He must, for example, be accounted an upright man; for otherwise his arguments, however forcible, his illustrations however clear, his delivery however graceful, will all suffer under the withering influence of a want of confidence. Integrity of character is, indeed, the capital quality—the "wisdom better than rubies; and all things that may be desired are not to be compared with it."

He must have the requisite natural gifts, and these must be cultivated with care and assiduity; for no fertility of genius, no powers of voice, no volubility of tongue, no grace of gesture, can ever atone for the absence of culture and discipline. Labor is the price of eminence in the fields of eloquence, as in every other honorable vocation.

He must have full control of himself, and a becoming respect for the feelings of others; for whatever may be the honesty of his intentions, the discipline of his intellectual powers, the treasures of his mind, or the fascinations of his oratory, if his temper be bad, his manner assuming, or his tone dictatorial, his success, in any and every line of speaking, must be seriously hindered. There is a mysterious charm in good nature, a certain irresistible attraction in every evidence of modesty, benevolence, and forbearance, which, in a public assembly, is often found more effective far than the most commanding talents.

But, in addition to those general qualifications which the good debater has in common with genuine orators of every description, there are others that belong peculiarly to his position and circumstances. Several of these, being the most important, we shall here specify and commend to the reader's attention.

1. He must, then, first and last, always endeavor to gain the good will of his audience: remembering, that persuasion is the only power at his command, and that the will of the assembly is the ultimate tribunal. In orations of the demonstrative kind, the orator may, with no little confidence, put his trust in wit, in humor, in mere novelty, in beauty and sublimity of thought, in felicities of diction and in graceful postures and attitudes; for his hearers are, for the most part, in a mood to be pleased, and are not to be called upon by a decisive vote to determine the merits of his performance. In speeches of the judicial kind, the speaker is fully justified in relying solely upon the making out of his case. If that which is alleged, is fully proved, he is

entitled to a verdict in favor of his client, and neither judge nor jury have either right or power to deny it.

But it is not so in deliberative bodies. The deliberative orator often addresses those who are well, or ill affected towards a cause, because they are well, or ill affected towards him who advocates it. And, since it is altogether optional with them to adopt, or reject what he recommends, it is of the utmost importance, that he should not lose the influence that ever accompanies a speaker who is regarded with kindness by his auditory.

2. He should be quick to discern those motives most likely to sway his auditors; otherwise his appeals will be powerless, because misdirected. There is a passage in the dialogue between Cicero and his son, quite pertinent to the present occasion, which, says a great and good man,* "I recommend, as the truly paternal advice of a father to his child." The passage is this: "The discourse must be accommodated, not only to the truth, but to the taste of the hearers. Observe, then, first of all, that there are two different descriptions of men; the one rude and ignorant, who always set profit before honor; the other polished and civilized, who prefer honor to everything. Urge, then, to the latter of these classes considerations of praise, of honor, of glory, of fidelity, of justice; in short, of every virtue. To the former present images of gain, of emolument, of thrift; nay, in addressing this kind of men, you must even allure them with the bait of pleasure. Pleasure, always hostile to virtue, always corrupting, by fraudulent imita-

* John Quncy Adams.

tion, the very nature of goodness herself, is yet most eagerly pursued by the worst of men; and by them often preferred not only to every instigation of honor, but even to the dictates of necessity. Remember, too, that mankind are more anxious to escape evil, than to obtain good; less eager to acquire honor, than to avoid shame. Who ever sought honor, glory, praise, or fame of any kind, with the same ardor that we fly from those most cruel of afflictions, ignominy, contumely, and scorn? Again; there is a class of men, naturally inclined to honorable sentiments, but corrupted by evil education and vitiated opinions. Is it your purpose, then, to exhort or persuade, remember that the task before you is that of teaching how to obtain good, and eschew evil. Are you speaking to men of liberal education, enlarge upon topics of praise and honor; insist with the keenest earnestness upon those virtues which contribute to the common safety and advantage of mankind. But, if you are discoursing to gross, ignorant, untutored minds, to them hold up profit, lucre, money-making, pleasure, and escape from pain. Deter them, also, by the prospect of shame and ignominy; for no man, however insensible to positive glory, is made of such impenetrable stuff, as not to be vehemently moved by the dread of infamy and disgrace."

To the same end, Quinctilian observes: "Now, there is no difficulty in persuading the virtuous to follow virtuous measures. But, if we are to plead for such measures before men of abandoned principles, we are carefully to avoid all appearance of reproaching them for the contrariety that there is between the measures and their character. For we are not then to think of winning their assent by expatiating upon the beauty of virtue, which never comes into the thoughts of such men; but we are to work upon them by the glory and the popularity that will attend their pursuing such a measure; and, if they look upon those but as empty sounds, we are then to lay before them the great profit which will thereby arise to themselves, and to magnify the dangers which may attend their doing otherwise. For the more worthless man is, the more susceptible he is of fear; nay, I am not sure whether the generality of mankind are not more influenced by the dread of danger than the hope of advantage; so much more easily and naturally is mankind in general struck with the notion of what is mean, than of what is noble."

In acting upon this advice of the great Roman orator, and the scarcely less great Roman Rhetorician, it need hardly be said, since the limitation will be obvious from the nature of the case, that the young orator is not advised to appeal to the motives of his hearers, whether high or low, in order to urge upon them what is wrong, but that having what he believes to be a good object, he may appeal to any and every suitable motive to influence men to seek that object.

3. He should be a man of general intelligence. This is true undoubtedly of orators in every line; but the remark has peculiar force and significance, when made in reference to him who desires to figure well in a deliberative assembly.

If we consider the multiplicity and diversity of the subjects acted upon in bodies of this kind, we can hardly estimate the importance of wide general information in a debater. With him no kind, or item of knowledge, is without a practical value. To-day he may be in a village meeting, discussing the expediency of making a road or building a bridge; tomorrow in a convention, arguing the propriety or impropriety of a change in the constitution of the State. Now he is busy among the friends of education, assembled to consider the ways and means of improving the moral and intellectual condition of the masses; now he is in some ecclesiastical synod, or council, or convocation, exchanging counsels on matters of high religious concernment; and now, again, perchance in Congress, debating questions of law, of tariff, of revenue, of treaties, of peace, of war, and I know not what all.

To him therefore, what knowledge or learning can be otherwise than exceedingly useful? To him history is indeed "philosophy teaching by examples;" yielding him arguments, facts, and illustrations, always interesting and often irresistible. To him not only is that history useful, which is embodied in permanent and well-digested records, but that, also, which is found in the passing events and transactions of the great living world around him. With him, in a sense singularly significant, "knowledge is power."

4. He should aim at simplicity of style, clearness of logic, and earnestness of manner. He may not discard ornament, when it comes naturally, but he is never to be found in search of it. His task is simply to show that something is to be sought, because it is useful, or that something is to be avoided, because it is deleterious.

The debater, therefore, must speak plainly, earnestly, feelingly; he must argue in the manner of a friend, intent upon guarding his neighbor against coming evil, or anxious to secure to him some blessing within the reach of effort.

In relation to the thought, he cannot be too careful; in relation to the mere wording of his thoughts, he must not seem over-anxious. If he is familiar with his theme, he will most probably be fluent in discussing it, and fluency of speech is what especially he needs. But fluency is not finery.

When the subject and the occasion conspire, as often they will, to render the use of ornate diction and figures of speech appropriate and effective, the deliberative orator is at liberty to rise with his topic and soar in the regions of beauty and sublimity. But let him beware of what is called beauty and sublimity of language, where there is no underlying beauty and sublimity of thought.

5. He should endeavor to have his thoughts and feelings so absorbed in his theme, as to free his delivery from every appearance of being studied and artificial. He that fully understands and ardently feels the force of what he is saying, will seldom be in danger of employing false tones and emphases, or awkward and inappropriate gestures. In these things nature is the best guide.

It will not be understood from this, that we would discourage all attention to vocal modulation, to justness of pronunciation, to proper gesticulation, and whatever else may constitute the requisites of a graceful delivery. These are things which, in every considerate mind, will always have their due weight.

But the error against which we would earnestly caution the young speaker, is that of withdrawing his attention, while speaking, from his subject to himself, busying his mind with the probable effect of his tones or his attitudes, when he ought to be dealing heartily with those emotions and sentiments on which, and on which alone, a truly natural delivery depends.

In this connection, we cannot resist the disposition to introduce an extract from a writer, whose opinion in a matter like this, is entitled to the highest consideration. It will serve equally for instruction and for encouragement. "He," (says Whately, the able and eloquent Archbishop of Dublin,) "who shall determine to aim at the natural manner, though he will have to contend with considerable difficulties and discouragements, will not be without corresponding advantages, in the course he is pursuing. He will be at first, indeed, repressed to a greater degree than another by emotions of bashfulness; but it will be more speedily and more completely subdued; the very system pursued, since it forbids all thoughts of *self*, striking at the root of the evil. He will, indeed, on the outset, incur censure, not only critical, but moral; he will be blamed for using a *colloquial* delivery; and the censure will very likely be, as far as relates to his earliest efforts, not wholly undeserved; for his manner *will* probably at first too much resemble that of conversation, though of serious and earnest conversation; but by perseverance he may be sure of avoiding deserved, and of mitigating, and ultimately overcoming, undeserved censure.

"He will, indeed, never be praised for a 'very fine delivery;' but his *matter* will not lose the approbation it may deserve; as he will be the more sure of being heard and attended to. He will not, indeed, meet with many who can be regarded as models of the natural manner; and those he does meet with, he will be precluded, by the nature of the system, from minutely imitating; but he will have the advantage of carrying within him an *infallible guide*, as long as he is careful to follow the suggestions of nature; abstaining from all thoughts respecting his own utterance, and fixing his mind intently on the business he is engaged in.

"And though he must not expect to attain perfection at once, he may be assured that, while he steadily adheres to this plan, he is in the right road to it; instead of becoming, as on the other plan, more and more artificial the longer he studies. And every advance he makes will produce a proportional effect; it will give him more and more of that hold on the attention, the understanding, and the feelings of the audience, which no studied modulation can ever attain. Others, indeed, may be more successful in escaping censure, and ensuring admiration; but he will far more surpass them in respect of the proper object of the orator, which is, *to carry his point.*"

6. The next special qualification for a good debater, here to be mentioned, is perfect familiarity with the rules of parliamentary practice. The necessity of such a code of laws is apparent from the nature of the case, and the wisdom of those now generally in force is fully attested by the voice of experience.

It not unfrequently happens, that the most important advantages in the management of a question are entirely lost through the speaker's ignorance of some form of procedure, or the operation and effect of some rule of order.

In the event of one's being elected to preside over the deliberations of a meeting or society, nothing can exceed the wasting, exhausting, mortifying process of laboring to govern and direct without knowing how.

On the contrary, if qualified in this respect, whether he figure on the floor in the capacity of a debater, or occupy the chair of the presiding officer, the order of proceeding, being fully understood, is made subservient to its legitimate purposes, the dignity of the assembly is duly maintained, and the interests at stake in the discussion carefully protected and promoted.

7. Last of all, as, indeed, first of all, he must be a good extemporaneous speaker. This, in fact, has all along been implied, and is absolutely essential to the character of a good debater.

Let no one, however, on this account be discouraged; as though nature had thrown in his way obstacles insurmountable. Excellency of speech is no exclusive gift of genius; but always, *more* or *less*, the fruit of practice. This fact is so important as to call for a separate consideration, and, accordingly, the following Section is devoted to that subject alone.

SECTION III.

EXTEMPORANEOUS SPEAKING.

TWO opinions, equally plausible and equally erroneous, are entertained in relation to extemporaneous speaking. One is, that this power, wherever possessed, in any eminent degree, is the peculiar gift of nature, and, therefore, absolutely unattainable, except by a favored few. The other is, that whether natural or acquired, confined to a few, or accessible to all, its frequent exercise is not only attended with no adequate benefit, but is, generally speaking, a positive injury; since it generates in the speaker himself habits unfavorable to close thinking and accurate composition.

The error underlying the first of these opinions seems to be, that of confounding two things essentially distinct—*thinking* and *speaking*. He that carefully attends to the operations of his own mind, will not be long in discovering, that when he speaks confusedly and obscurely, there is in his thoughts, at the time, a correspondent want of order and clearness.

This confusion and obscurity of thought may be due to a variety of causes. It is not always traceable to ignorance of the subject, to want of premeditation, or to an ill-disciplined mind; though these will be found to be the real causes of almost all abortive attempts at extemporaneous speaking.

Many a man who has a complete mastery of his subject, and who, in the retirement of his study, would readily clothe his thoughts upon it in appropriate and even elegant language, finds in the mere presence of a numerous audience an overpowering cause of derangement in his ideas, and a consequent inability to deliver a connected discourse. This result is sometimes experienced from the presence of particular individuals whom we dread as critics, sometimes from a contemptuous bearing in our opponents,* sometimes from an overweening vanity in the speaker himself, rendering him over-solicitous about the appearance he is making in the assembly, sometimes— But further enumeration is unnecessary. It is enough that the sources of

* A striking instance of this kind is recorded of Lord Erskine. In the commencement of his maiden speech in the House of Commons, "Pitt," says Croly in his Life of George IV., "evidently intending to reply, sat with pen and paper in his hand, prepared to catch the arguments of his formidable adversary. He wrote a word or two. Erskine proceeded; but, with every additional sentence, Pitt's attention to the paper relaxed, his look became more careless, and he obviously began to think the orator less and less worthy of his attention. At length, while every eye in the House was fixed upon him, with a contemptuous smile he dashed the pen through the paper, and flung them on the floor. Erskine never recovered from this expression of disdain; his voice faltered, he struggled through the remainder of his speech, and sank into his seat dispirited."

Thus Erskine, an orator of pre-eminent ability at the bar, whom talents of the highest order in an opponent would rather have encouraged than disheartened, was utterly disconcerted by the power of *contempt*.

failure in all these and similar cases, lie, not in the absence of natural endowment, but in causes quite removable by care, study and effort.

In asserting, however, that the power of extemporizing is the gift, not of a few only, but rather of the race generally, we are, by no means, to be understood as affirming the natural *equality* of all mankind in this respect. Indeed, the great *in*equality found among men, in facility of expression, is what gives plausibility to the opinion, that while some few possess it in a high degree, to the many it is altogether denied.

What we hold is, that all are, by nature, in possession of this faculty; that it is, nevertheless, more prominent in some than in others; but that, like all other faculties, it is capable of indefinite improvement. *What* a man understands and *as* he understands, he will be able to express; whether gracefully or awkwardly, forcibly or feebly, elegantly or otherwise, depends more upon previous culture and discipline than upon any natural endowments whatever.

The history of eloquence, in all ages and countries, teems with examples in favor of the position, that not only the power of extemporaneous speech, but all the other qualities engaged in the composition of a genuine orator, derive their perfection from study and practice. Such was the confidence of the celebrated Gorgias Leontinus in the efficacy of mental training, as the means of forming a fluent speaker, that he did not hesitate to pledge himself to qualify his pupils to speak extemporaneously on any subject whatever.

Undoubtedly his pretensions were too high. Doubtless he deserved much of the ridicule heaped upon him by Plato. But, after all, we must remember, that he was a man of extraordinary ability, that Plato was his rival, and, moreover, that both in Rhetoric, which unfolds the principles, and in Oratory, which displays the practice of speaking well, he was confessedly pre-eminent. His testimony, therefore, in the matter under consideration, must be regarded as decidedly valuable.*

The toils and trials of Demosthenes in the effort to overcome the obstacles lying in his way to oratorical eminence, are familiar to every reader of ancient history. What he did, and what he suffered, and what, finally, he came to be, in consequence of thus doing and suffering, taken all together, serve admirably to show, among other things, the true *source* of skill in extemporaneous speaking. Demosthenes was, indeed, for the most part, laborious in his preparations; so much so as to elicit from Pytheas, one of his rivals, and from others, the taunting remark, that "*all his arguments smelled of the lamp.*"† But, when the occasion demand-

* None of the early rhetoricians had a wider reputation than Gorgias. Among his pupils was the celebrated Isocrates; from whose school, says Cicero, as from the Trojan horse, issued a host of heroes. When sent by his countrymen, the Leontinians, at the head of an embassy, to seek the alliance of Athens against the encroachments of Syracuse, Gorgias so charmed the Athenians by the power of his eloquence, that he found no difficulty in securing the end of his mission. All Greece, it is said, united in erecting a golden statue of him in the temple at Delphi.

† It is recorded of Demosthenes by his distinguished biographer, that he held it to be a duty which he owed to the people, not, as a general thing, to undertake to address them, without duly considering beforehand what he should say. Of Pericles, also, the same writer says, that "such was his solicitude, when he had to speak in public, that he always first addressed a prayer to the gods, 'that not a word might unawares escape him unsuitable to the occasion.'" The

ed, he had a habit of mind, derived from the severe discipline to which it had been subjected, which enabled him, upon the spur of the moment, "to speak," says Plutarch, "as from a supernatural impulse," and equally to delight and instruct by his extemporaneous effusions.

In modern times, also, numerous cases have occurred in which, after decided failures in the first attempts at extemporaneous discourse, men have, by resolution and perseverance, equally surprised themselves and their friends in the success which has attended their efforts in this direction. It is well known that even Sheridan, from whom so much was expected, on account of the brilliancy of his career in another sphere, came, in his first speech in the House of Commons, amazingly short of those anticipations that had been raised in relation to the figure he would make in a deliberative assembly. But his reply to Woodfall, whose opinion he had solicited respecting the merit of this his first attempt, and who frankly told him, "*I don't think this is your line: you had better have stuck to your former pursuits*," is one that announces, with peculiar force, the truth which we are here anxious to impress. "It is *in* me," said he, "and it shall come *out* of me!" And come *out* of him it did; for at it he went, with something of Demosthenian spirit, and his perseverance was ultimately crowned with something of Demosthenian success.

This declaration and resolution of Sheridan, so briefly and so forcibly expressed, should arrest the at-

conduct of these great men, in this respect, is, or ought to be, not a little instructive. Especially should it be remembered, that their solicitude was chiefly about the *thoughts*, not about the *words*.

tention of every young man, who finds himself vacillating between hope and fear in his aspirations after oratorical ability. Let him accept, with unwavering faith, the doctrine taught in the first clause,—"It is *in* me;" let him take with cool deliberation the resolve expressed in the second,—"and it shall come *out* of me;" and, thereafter, let neither zeal flag, nor energy fail, nor perseverance yield, till that which is *within*, shall have shown itself *without* in the form of a ready and effective debater.

In relation to the second opinion, cited at the commencement of this section, and there pronounced erroneous, it should, in the outset, be observed, that whatever influence extemporaneous speaking may be supposed to have in producing habits of indolence, or inaccuracy, it is certain that the practice of writing out discourses beforehand is no necessary safeguard against these unfortunate tendencies. He that is habitually careful and diligent, is not likely to have his habits broken up, but rather strengthened by the exercise of his powers, as an extemporaneous orator; while he, in whom carelessness and idleness have fixed their abode, has in him two evil spirits, too powerful to be exorcised by the mere practice of penmanship.

Written speeches ought, we should say, to give infallible evidence always of care and assiduity; but he is certainly a listless looker-on in any of the various fields of public speaking, who is not often forced to wonder how people who evidently think so loosely and so lazily, can ever prevail upon themselves to undergo the mechanical exertion necessary to write out a speech. Men often write what is not worth writing, just as they often speak what is not worth speaking.

Extemporaneous speaking is not, therefore, to be discouraged, because some persons seem, by the practice of it, to acquire habits of idleness and carelessness in the matter of literary composition. Rather let it be the more earnestly cultivated, in order to the avoidance of these very evils; for, when well executed, it assuredly argues higher and better culture, and consequently, greater industry and accuracy, than belongs, or ever can belong, to the race of literary drones.

But the opinion which we are here combating, however erroneous, is certainly plausible. Its plausibility, moreover, is due, undoubtedly, to the experienced fact, that those speakers who are in the habit of seeking improvement in the power of expression, by exercising themselves often in written composition, are always found to be the most ready and effective extemporizers. This testimony in favor of the influence of written upon oral exercises in composition, we cheerfully accept, and cannot find language strong enough to commend it to those who are ambitious to excel as debaters; for we are here only guarding people against the error of supposing that, because writing conduces, in the highest degree, to accuracy in composition, that, therefore, extemporaneous speaking is to be relinquished altogether. Indeed, one of the most valuable precepts for the acquisition of skill in extemporizing, as we shall presently see, is systematic practice in reducing our thoughts to writing.

But our object, in this part of the present work, is not so much to consider and refute objections to the practice of declaiming extemporaneously, as to offer suitable directions for the cultivation of that useful art. We hasten, therefore, to direct attention to the following precepts; not, however, as embracing every item of instruction applicable to the case, but simply as embodying the most prominent and available guidance in this line of intellectual exertion.

In delivering these instructions, it is of course assumed, that the party receiving them has an earnest desire to become a good extemporaneous speaker, and is, therefore, willing and ready, as far as may be practicable, to follow them out in a spirit of zeal and perseverance. This is an indispensable preliminary to any sort of success in the matter; for no idle aspirations, no lazy wishes, unaccompanied by resolution and industry, can ever achieve a position worth occupying in the arena of public debate.

The first rule which we shall here lay down, as conducive, if rightly followed, to skill in the use of extemporaneous language, is—*Endeavor always to think clearly and methodically.*

Thinking and speaking, as before intimated, are things correlative. They stand in the relation of cause and effect. When, therefore, it is the settled habit of the mind to think in an orderly and perspicuous manner, it follows naturally that the tongue, which is under the guidance of the mind, should utter words in a corresponding style.

In order to the efficient application of this rule, let the young speaker often assume, as an intellectual gymnastic, some debatable subject for the exercise of his mental powers. Let him then deal with it as with a thing of reality, a question of real life. Let him acquire an interest, an enthusiasm, if possible, in its management. Let him survey it as a whole, study it in detail, detect its deficiencies, bring out its excellencies, and hold it up to the light in all possible aspects. Let him consider in how many ways the point which he wishes to make can be presented and defended, and, among these, which is the most likely to be fully understood, and fairly appreciated.

When all this is done in the mind, let him try the experiment of putting the whole process into extemporaneous language. The result will be the measure of his proficiency in the art; and, if rightly regarded, cannot fail, at every repetition of the exercise, to prove a healthful stimulus to renewed exertion.

The second rule is—*Be in the constant habit of seeking the best possible language for the expression of your ideas, even in ordinary conversation.*

As the best school of practical morals is the society of moral people, so the best exercise in oral expression is conversation with refined and educated persons. The converse of this statement is also painfully true. "Evil communications corrupt good manners," says the Apostle; and some one has aptly added—"*and good language too!*"

He, therefore, who aims to be a good deliberative orator, must be ever equally on the alert to catch what is choice and correct, and to avoid what is vulgar and inaccurate, in his daily intercourse with others. It is not enough to exercise particular care on particular occasions. It must be a thing of habit, growing out of a settled purpose to be superior in the power of speech.

The third rule is—*Read often and carefully the best specimens of deliberative eloquence.*

An intelligent application of this rule requires that the student should become familiar with many particulars bearing upon what he reads. What is the precise nature of the proposition which the speaker advocates or opposes? What are his own personal relations to it? What is the character or constitution of the body whom he addresses? What the time, the place, the circumstances, wherein the speech was delivered? All these and other kindred inquiries he should make, in order to put himself duly in sympathy with the parties originally and really interested in the case.

Then let him observe accurately the speech itself; its opening, the order and relative force of the several arguments adduced, the skill displayed in evading or obviating objections, the pertinency of the illustrations, the facility and naturalness of the transitions from one topic to another, the closing remarks or peroration, and, throughout the whole, every grace and every elegance in the structure of individual sentences or passages.

The fourth rule is—*Exercise your powers often in the practice of written composition.*

"Writing," says Lord Bacon, "makes an accurate man," and this is the testimony of every scholar. The rule, however, which we are now commending, has several modes of application. If the student is acquainted with any language other than his vernacular, one of the easiest applications of the present rule is the translating of passages out of that foreign language into his own. Every sentence thus translated is an exercise, however brief, in English composition; a fact which accounts for the greater facility in the use of language, which boys who have studied, even for comparatively short periods of time, the Latin and Greek languages, than is found in the possession of those who are without that advantage.

He, however, who knows no other than his native tongue, may adopt, with the greatest benefit, a custom, commended and adopted by Cicero and other great speakers, in their youth,—that of reading carefully a passage from some great oration or other literary composition, getting the substance of it fairly in the memory, and then putting it again into language the best you can command. There is, also, another way of reaching the result contemplated in this exercise, which the author of these observations has often found singularly efficient, in the prosecution of his duties as a practical educator. It is simply to place before the learner a given passage from a writer of established reputation, and then to require him to express, in words other than those of the author, the same idea; that is, neither more nor less than what is found in the passage assigned. This is an admirable method of acquiring precision of style, on which depends, in great measure, every other excellence of composition.

But a higher application of the present rule for the cultivation of skill in speaking, is that which obliges the young orator to engage frequently in the practice of original composition. In this, if he would be proficient, he must study to bring into actual and appropriate use those essential principles and precepts which, under the imposing names of Grammar and Rhetoric, all terminate at last in justifying that brief definition of a good style,—"proper words in proper places."

By the due application of this rule, whether in one or in all of the ways above indicated, the mind becomes habituated to close and accurate thinking, familiar with various forms of expression, and ready, when the occasion demands, to display its resources in fluent and forceful language.

The fifth and last general rule which we shall here give for acquiring superiority in extemporaneous speaking, is—*Be always diligent in the acquisition of knowledge.*

The aim of this rule is especially to reach the case of those who, relying upon a certain natural readiness of utterance, are but too apt to fall into the deplorable habit of undertaking to speak without having anything in particular to say. He that fails from this cause, deserves to fail; for he equally deceives himself and his audience; mistaking sound for sense, and raising expectations which he is not able to satisfy. A glib tongue in an empty head is no common calamity.

There is no kind of knowledge, as before intimated, which may not be useful to the deliberative speaker. Such is the variety of the questions which he may find it necessary or desirable to discuss, that no mental treasures, however extensive or diversified, can exceed the limits of his actual wants.

It was no mere fancy that led the ancients to adopt the principle, that the genuine orator should be competently acquainted with every department of knowledge. Not that, even in their day, the orator could be expected to be a man of universal knowledge, in any such sense as includes and necessitates a minute and profound acquaintance with all the various and complicated branches of human learning. This, if not then, certainly now, would be quite out of human power; but there is an important sense in which this theory of universal culture is unquestionably true. Let the standard be high, whatever may be our deficiencies in reaching it.

The perfect orator is, indeed, the rarest of human characters. It is seldom, in the lapse of ages, that all those qualities that must conspire to produce this character are found to unite in a single individual. In voice, in person, in genius, in knowledge, in fluency, in everything that can influence the eye, the ear, the heart, or the head, he must be pre-eminent.

Few, therefore, very few, can ever hope to attain to the glory of being perfect orators; but all, or nearly all, by persevering and judicious practice, may become ready and efficient speakers.

"But," as is well observed by an eminent writer,* already quoted, "no man ought to place such confidence in his own abilities as to hope to rise to the highest pitch of reputation by his first efforts. For our extemporary powers of speaking must rise by degrees, from inconsiderable beginnings to perfection. *And this can neither be acquired nor maintained without practice.*"

* Quinctillian.

SECTION IV.

RULES OF ORDER IN DELIBERATIVE ASSEMBLIES.

THIS part of the present work embraces a pretty full course of instruction in the Rules of Order observed in deliberative assemblies. For reasons elsewhere* assigned, these rules deservedly claim the most careful attention.

They are, indeed, of almost universal applicability; but (as stated on page 41) are often, by special rules, altered, modified, or superseded, in certain points, to answer the demands of particular organizations.

In this part of the subject, moreover, we have adopted the mode of question and answer. This has been done, partly, because it seemed more likely to elicit attention, and, partly, because, where the work is employed as a text-book, such an arrangement can hardly fail to prove highly convenient and useful.

Those who may wish merely to refer to particular points, in this or any other part of the work, will be able readily to reach their object, by means of the Index at the end, which has been made, expressly for that purpose, very full and minute.

* See page 40.

PRELIMINARY INSTRUCTIONS.

1. *What is a deliberative assembly?*

A deliberative assembly is an organized meeting of persons convened to consider and examine the reasons for and against measures and propositions submitted for their decision.

2. *What is meant by an "organized" meeting?*

To organize is to form, or supply with the proper *organs*, that is, with the *means* or *instruments* of action; and, when applied to an assemblage of persons gathered for deliberation, signifies to supply with suitable officers, and otherwise so to provide, that all the members may duly participate in the proceedings

3. *What officers are necessary for a deliberative assembly?*

The officers necessary for a deliberative body are a Presiding Officer* and a Secretary or Clerk; but others may be appointed, according to the exigencies of the occasion, or the special nature of the organization. Thus, there may be one or more Vice-Presidents, one

* The presiding officer in a deliberative body is variously denominated. In the Senate of the United States, he is the *President;* in the House of Representatives, he is the *Speaker;* in certain ecclesiastical organizations, he is the *Moderator;* in ordinary meetings, resulting from a published call, he is styled the *Chairman. President* is the name most comprehensive, and the one most commonly employed in literary and other societies, in Boards of Managers, and in other similar organizations.

or more additional Secretaries, a Corresponding Secretary and a Treasurer.

4. *Are the proceedings, in a deliberative assembly, conducted in accordance with any particular rules?*

All business in deliberative bodies is transacted in conformity with certain rules and regulations, which experience has shown to be fit and necessary for that purpose. These are called Rules of Order.

5. *What is the particular advantage of rules of order?*

The object of a meeting for deliberation is, of course, to obtain a free expression of opinion, and a fair decision of the questions discussed. Without rules of order, this object would, in most cases, be utterly defeated; for there would be no uniformity in the modes of proceeding, no restraint upon indecorous or disorderly conduct, no protection to the rights and privileges of members, no guarantee against the caprices and usurpations of a presiding officer, no safeguard against tyrannical majorities, nor any suitable regard to the rights of a minority.

6. *Are the rules of order alike in all deliberative assemblies?*

The rules of order in our National Congress are essentially the same as those in force in the British Parliament; being, in fact, mainly derived from that source. There are, however, important differences; growing chiefly out of differences in government and institutions.

The rules of order in our State Legislatures are substantially the same as those adopted in the National Congress; being, indeed, founded thereupon. But, as the rules in use in Congress differ, in some respects, from those established in Parliament, so those in the several State Legislatures differ, in some particulars, from those adopted in Congress.

And again, as the rules in the several State Legislatures differ, in some points, from those in Congress, on which they are founded, so do they differ not unfrequently from one another; though in all the essentials of the common code, they are quite in harmony.

The rules of order in most other deliberative bodies in this country, are, in the main, the same with those in the National Congress or in the State Legislatures; so that, in almost all fundamental points, there is great uniformity of practice. Hence, in allusion to the origin of the code of rules and regulations, thus generally established, it is often called THE COMMON CODE OF PARLIAMENTARY LAW.

7. *Is it customary, in deliberative bodies, to adopt rules other than those embraced in this common code?*

It is not unusual for deliberative bodies of every kind, especially permanent organizations, to adopt, in addition to the common code, a series of special rules. These special rules, if, in any particular, they conflict with the ordinary parliamentary laws, always, so far as the body that adopts them is concerned, take the precedence. Where there is no special rule, there, of course, the common law is to be enforced.

8. *In what form are the acts of a deliberative assembly usually expressed?*

The decisions or resolves of a deliberative assembly, which properly constitute their *acts*, are usually embodied and affirmed in formal declarations, called Resolutions.

These resolutions are on motion duly seconded, and stated from the chair, first freely discussed, and then decided affirmatively, or negatively by the meeting.

9. *What is meant by the phrase "on motion, duly seconded"?*

Whenever a member wishes to get the sense, or judgment of the body on any given proposition, and, for that purpose, moves, or proposes its adoption, he is said to make a motion.

To *move* a resolution, therefore, is simply to offer it for consideration. But it can never be entertained by the meeting, unless it so far finds favor, that some member other than the proposer, gives it his sanction by becoming his second.

To *second* a motion, then, is to join with the proposer thereof, as his aid or *second*, in offering it to the consideration of the meeting. The party moving the resolution introduces it with, or without previous remarks, by saying: "*Mr. President, I beg leave to offer the following Resolution;*" which he then reads aloud. The party seconding, simply says: "*I second that motion.*"

10. *Are not the words "motion" and "resolution" often convertible terms?*

Motion, literally means *the act* of moving; resolution,

the act of resolving; but these words, like all others of the same formation, may signify, respectively, either the *act* of moving, or that which *is* moved, the *act* of resolving, or that which *is* resolved. Hence, since that which is moved, or proposed, in a deliberative body often proves identical with that which is resolved, these two words are generally regarded as synonymous. The distinction, however, between them deserves to be kept in mind, and it may further serve to impress it, if we remember, that while it is quite common and proper to say, "*I move a resolution*," it would be wholly inadmissible to reverse the terms and say, "*I resolve a motion.*" *

11. *In what way or ways are decisions commonly made in a deliberative assembly?*

The decisions in a deliberative assembly are commonly made by open vote; often, also, by ballot.

There is also another mode of taking the question, which is called, taking the question by *yeas* and *nays.*

12. *What is the difference between a vote and a ballot?*

Vote, literally means a *vow*, *wish* or *will.* It is,

* Mathias (Rules of Order, p. 44) mentions a distinction made in Legislative bodies between these two terms, which rests, as will be seen, essentially upon the original differences of import indicated in the text. He says: "Legislative bodies make a marked distinction between resolutions and motions. The former are presumed to embrace matters of importance, and, after being read by the clerk, require a motion to 'proceed to a second reading and consideration.' Motions are of minor character, and relate generally to order in taking up business, or to some preparatory movements necessary for business. These do not require a second reading."

therefore, properly used to signify the choice, or preference, which one may have along with others, in relation to matters submitted for decision or persons proposed for office. This choice, or preference may be signified in different ways. It may be made *viva voce* (with the living voice); it may be made by raising the hand; and, besides various other ways, by *ballot.*

Ballot, primarily, signifies a *little ball;* and to vote by ballot is properly to signify one's choice by throwing into a box, urn, or other receptacle, a ball so colored, or otherwise marked, as to indicate an affirmative or negative vote. Instead of ballots, however, tickets, as being more convenient, are now generally used, though the process is still called by the same name.

13. *What proportion of the votes given in any case, is necessary to determine a question?*

The number of votes necessary to determine a question, where there is no special rule to the contrary, is always a majority. But, in certain cases, other proportions are required, as two-thirds or three-fourths; or, as is sometimes the case, a mere plurality.

14. *What difference, in speaking of the result of a vote or election, is there between the terms majority and plurality?*

Majority signifies *the* greater part, that is, more than half. He, therefore, that is elected by a majority, is elected by more than half of all the votes cast.

Plurality signifies *a* greater number; that is (in the case, for example, of an election where there are more than two candidates), a number greater than that received by any other candidate, but less than half of the whole number of votes cast. Thus, a candidate may have a plurality without having a majority; but he cannot have a majority without having a plurality.

15. *Must a motion submitted for the decision of a deliberative assembly, be oral or written?*

Every motion calling for special care and deliberation, that is, all important motions, should be in writing; but motions merely affecting the order of business, or other subordinate matters, are usually oral.

16. *What differences in meaning or application, if any, are found to obtain among the words "Voted," "Ordered," and "Resolved," when placed at the beginning of propositions adopted by deliberate assemblies?*

Whatever proposition has been duly adopted by a deliberative assembly, thereby becomes the *vote*, *order*, or *resolution* of that assembly. The terms "*Voted*," "*Ordered*," and "*Resolved*," therefore, are in so far synonymous, as they all properly indicate what has been *done* or *decided* upon.

"*Resolved*," however, is the term most generally used: "*Voted*" being employed, it is said, chiefly in the Eastern States, while "*Ordered*" is confined mainly to religious organizations.*

*** Hatsell (quoted in Jefferson's Manual, section xxi.) says:—When the House commands, it is "an order." But facts, principles, their own opinions and purposes, are expressed in the form of resolutions.**

17. *Why and when is a proposition before a deliberative body called a question?*

When, after due deliberation, a motion comes to be put to vote, that is, when the question of its acceptance or rejection is directly submitted to the assembly, it is, then and for that reason, called *the question.*

18. *What form is observed in submitting a question?*

When the debate, or deliberation upon a subject appears to be at a close, the presiding officer simply asks: "*Is the assembly ready for the question?*"

If no one signifies a desire further to discuss or consider the subject, he then proceeds to submit the question thus: "*As many as are in favor of the adoption of the Resolution, will signify it by saying 'Aye!'*" Then, pausing a moment to hear the response, he adds: "*Those of the contrary opinion will say 'No!'*"

The answer on both sides being duly given, the President announces the result; saying, "*The ayes have it,*" or "*The noes have it,*" according as he finds the one or the other side in the majority.

Should there seem to be any doubt about the result, the President should say: "The ayes *appear* to have it." If then no dissatisfaction is manifested, or no division called for, he adds: "The ayes *have* it."

19. *Suppose, after the vote is given, the president is unable to decide, or after he has announced the result, his decision is questioned, what should be done?*

Should the president, after putting the question, (if necessary a second time,) still be unable to decide, or should his decision, when announced, be brought into question by a member rising in his place, and calling for a division of the house, his duty is immediately to so divide, or arrange the assembly as to allow the votes on each side to be accurately counted.

This may be done by directing the ayes and the noes respectively to take different sides of the room; or by first requesting the ayes to stand up in their places long enough to be numbered, and then calling upon the noes to do the same thing; or by asking the ayes each to raise the right hand, and as soon as those have been counted, inviting the noes to signify their will in the like manner.

Whatever method be adopted, the President is to count, or appoint tellers to count, the votes on each side respectively, and announce the true result to the assembly.

20. *Suppose the members are equally divided, what follows?*

If, on any question, the members are equally divided, the President must give the casting, or determining vote.

21. *Has any member a right to refrain from voting?*

Every member present at the time when a question is duly submitted to the assembly for decision, is bound to give his vote for, or against the pending proposition.*

22. *What is meant by taking a question by the yeas and nays?*

It is sometimes thought proper to record the names

* In some deliberative bodies, members are excused at their own request from voting; but this is clearly against duty in the case.

of members in connection with the votes they give for or against a proposition. In order to this, the question is thus stated: "*As many as are in favor of the resolution* (or whatever it is) *will, as their names are called, answer 'Yes;' and as many as are opposed to it, will answer 'No.'*"

The roll is then called by the Clerk, or Secretary, and as each member answers *yes*, or *no*, the answer is noted or marked opposite his name; and, to afford opportunity for the correction of mistakes, if any, the names of the voters on each side are again read over, and then the result is formally declared by the President. This is what is called taking a vote by yeas and nays.*

* The method of taking the yeas and nays in the House of Representatives in the State of Massachusetts, as described by Mr. Cushing, is so simple and so satisfactory, as to commend itself to every one. "The names of the members," says he, "being printed on a sheet, the clerk calls them in their order; and, as each one answers, the clerk (responding to the member at the same time) places a figure in pencil, expressing the number of the answer, at the left or right of the name, according as the answer is yes or no; so that the last figure or number, on each side, shows the number of the answers on that side; and the two last numbers or figures represent the respective numbers of the affirmatives and negatives on the division. Thus, at the left hand of the name of the member who first answers *yes*, the clerk places a figure 1; at the right hand of the first member who answers *no*, he also places a figure 1; the second member that answers *yes* is marked 2; and so on to the end of the list; the side of the name, on which the figure is placed, denoting whether the answer is *yes* or *no*, and the figure denoting the number of the answer on that side. The affirmatives and negatives are then read separately, if necessary, though this is usually omitted, and the clerk is then prepared, by means of the last figure on each side, to give the numbers to the Speaker to be announced to the House."

23. *Is it in order to re-open the discussion after the voting upon it has been commenced?*

A debatable question is always open for discussion in the assembly, both in the negative and the affirmative. And unless, therefore, the vote is taken by the yeas and nays, in which case both sides of the question are voted upon simultaneously, it is always in order, even after the affirmative has been put, to renew the debate.

24. *How can it affect the result to renew the discussion, seeing that one side has already voted?*

In case of a renewal of the debate after the affirmative has been put, the question, when again submitted, must be put both in the affirmative and the negative; for the new discussion may have brought new light, and, besides, members not present before may have since entered, and so long as the question remains under debate, every one has a right to a vote one way or the other, as he pleases.

25. *Suppose a difficulty arises during a division on some point of order, as, for example, whether a member has a right to vote, how is the matter to be disposed of?*

Should any difficulty on a point of order arise during a division, the President is to dispose of it by a peremptory decision; such decision, if improper, being afterwards subject to censure or correction.*

* He sometimes, however, in such cases, avails himself of the advice of experienced members; they keeping their seats to avoid the appearance of debate. But all this is at the pleasure of the President; otherwise the decision might be protracted beyond all reasonable bounds. See Jef. Manual, sec. xii., and Cushing, p. 131.

26. *If, while a decision is going on, the number of members present falls below that required for a quorum, does that hinder the decision of the question?*

If, on a division, the result of the count shows that the whole number of votes is not equal to that required for a quorum, no decision can be had. In that event the matter to be decided, remains just as it was before the decision was ordered or undertaken, and when resumed must be continued from that point, or stage of progress.

MODE OF ORGANIZING.

27. *What is the proper mode of organizing a meeting?*

The usual mode of organizing a meeting is for some one,* at the time appointed, to request the attention of the assembly present, and after suggesting the propriety of appointing a president, solicit nominations for that office. The nominations being made, he moves that the person first nominated be requested to preside over the deliberations of the meeting. If that be seconded, he says: "*Those in favor of this motion will please signify it by saying 'Aye!'*" The response to this being given, he adds: "*Those opposed to the motion will please say 'No!'*"

If the question be decided in the affirmative,† the

* If the meeting has been convened by a public call, or advertisement, it seems most proper that one of the persons signing the call should commence business by either nominating a person to preside, or soliciting nominations from the assembly. A call for a public meeting should always state clearly the object had in view, and be signed by the parties most prominent in originating it.

† If, however, the question be negatived, another nomination is,

person so elected immediately takes the chair, and proceeds to complete the organization, by requesting the members to nominate a suitable person for the office of Secretary, as also persons for such other offices as may be deemed necessary or expedient.

28. *Would it be in order to organize temporarily, for the purpose of effecting a permanent organization?*

It would not only be in order, but it is also sometimes very desirable to effect a temporary organization, for the express purpose of obtaining a judicious selection of officers. This is especially the case where the meeting is composed of persons from different and distant parts of the country, and who may not, consequently, be personally known to one another.

The mode of appointing a chairman and other officers *pro tem.*, is the same as that described (in answer to question 27) for the appointment of permanent officers.

29 *In what way does the meeting, thus temporarily organized, proceed to select suitable officers?*

It is customary, and, perhaps, always best, to refer the matter to a committee. The committee, in such case, should retire immediately, examine the claims of the several persons apparently suitable for the places to be filled, and, with all convenient dispatch, report a list of candidates to the meeting.*

30. *Suppose it should be the will of a meeting, called for*

of course, requested, and acted upon as before; and this process is repeated, if necessary, till a president is chosen.

* For the mode of presenting and receiving the Report of a Committee, see page 000.

a temporary purpose, to form itself into a regular society, what form should be observed in so doing?

A meeting, or convention convoked for a temporary object, may be converted into a permanent organization, by passing a resolution to that effect, and providing, also, by resolution, for the appointment of a committee to draft and report a constitution for the proposed society. The constitution, when duly accepted and adopted, should be signed by all the persons adopting it, and should fix the conditions, on which other persons might afterwards be admitted to membership.

DUTIES OF OFFICERS AND MEMBERS.

31. *What are the duties of the President?*

The ordinary duties of the President are the following:

(1.) To preside impartially over the deliberations of the assembly,—to enforce the rules of order in the transaction of business,—to be kind and courteous himself, and to maintain due decorum among the members,—to give information, when necessary, on points of order, and, in cases of dispute, to decide upon questions of Parliamentary practice:

(2.) To receive and duly announce all messages and communications for the assembly,—to insist upon a strict observance of the order of business,—to submit, in an orderly way, all proper motions, propositions or petitions made by members,—to see that each member has his just rights and privileges in debate,—to put to vote all questions that have been properly brought forward for discussion and decision, and officially make known the result.

(3.) To appoint by name, when so directed or required, the members that are to serve on committees,—to take measures, as far as may be, that such committees discharge efficiently the duties incumbent upon them; and at all meetings, whether stated or special, to call for their Reports, if due, and see that these are, in proper form, presented to the meeting:

(4.) To see, that the several other officers properly discharge the duties assigned to them,—that the requisitions of the Constitution and By-Laws be fully complied with,—that the instructions of the society on every occasion be rightly carried out,—that its acts and proceedings, when necessary, be duly authenticated by his signature; and, in short, that the true aims of the organization never be frustrated, either by his own, or the negligence of others.

32. *What is the duty of a Vice-President?*

The duty of the Vice-President is, in the absence of the President, to assume and transact all such business as properly falls within the province of the presidential office.

33. *What are the duties of the Recording Secretary?*

The duties of the Recording Secretary are, in general, these:

To call the roll at the opening of a meeting, and note the names of the members absent,—to record faithfully the doings of the society,—to read aloud such papers as may be ordered to be read,—to call the roll when the vote is taken by yeas and nays, and record the answer of each member,—to notify committees of their appointment and of the matters committed to them,—to authenticate, when necessary, by his signature, the acts and proceedings of the body, and to take in charge all papers and documents belonging thereto.

34. *What is the duty of a Corresponding Secretary?*

The duty of the Corresponding Secretary is to conduct, under the instructions of the society, all correspondence with other societies or individuals.

35. *What is the duty of the Treasurer?*

The duty of the Treasurer is to receive, and under specified regulations, to disburse all moneys belonging to the society,—to keep an accurate account of all pecuniary matters pertaining thereto,—and when required, to give a clear and correct statement of its financial condition.

36. *What are the rights of the members?*

Every member has an equal right with every other member, to offer in the proper way, any motion, or resolution which he may deem expedient,—to enter, in the way of explanation and discussion, upon the merits of his proposition, and to have it duly weighed and decided upon by the assembly. He has, also, in common with the rest, various other rights and privileges, which will come up more properly under other heads.

37. *What are the duties of the members?*

The duty of every member is to follow strictly the rules of order,—to abstain from all personalities in debate,—never designedly or heedlessly to interrupt another member while speaking,—never to create disturbance in the assembly, or any part thereof, by whispering, hissing, or any other act of indecency,—and, finally, in all respects to observe the decorum and propriety of deportment proper to a gentleman.

MODE OF COMMENCING BUSINESS.

38. *What is the first step after the organization of a meeting?*

The first step after organizing is for the President officially to announce, that the meeting being duly organized, is now ready for the transaction of business.

It is quite customary, moreover, for the President, upon taking his place as the presiding officer of a meeting, to make a short address suitable to the occasion. If the meeting be the result of a published call, he should read the call aloud, or himself state, in few words, the objects proposed by those who have made it.

39. *When the assembly is thus duly organized, and ready for business, how is it to be introduced?*

Business may be introduced in a deliberative assembly either by the presentation of petitions, memorials, or other papers, emanating from persons not belonging to the body, or by offering resolutions, or by calling for the Reports of Committees.

If the meeting has been called for some specific object, the proper course is for some one to rise and move that a Committee be appointed to draft Resolutions expressive of the sense of the assembly.

While the Committee are out, engaged in this duty, it is usual to call on some suitable person to address the meeting. As soon as he has closed his remarks, the Committee, if ready, immediately present their Report in the manner described on page 112.

In case Resolutions have been prepared beforehand, as sometimes happens, they are, of course, presented to the meeting in due form, without the intervention of a committee.

40. *How is business commenced at a meeting of a Society, or other permanent organization?*

The presiding officer, on taking his place, first requests the members to come to order. Then, either by counting himself, or directing the Secretary to call the roll, he proceeds to ascertain whether there is a *quorum* present.

If there be a quorum, he then requests the Secretary to read the minutes of the last meeting;* if not, business is, of course, suspended till the next regular meeting.

41. *What is meant by a quorum?*

A *quorum* is such a number of members as may, by rule, or statute, be required to be present at a meeting in order to render the transactions of the body legal, or valid. Thus, by the Constitution of the United States, it is provided, that a majority of each House of Congress shall be necessary to form a quorum to transact business.†

* For the mode of approving of the minutes, &c., &c., see page 110.

† The term *quorum* (literally, *of whom*) is one of the words used,

COMMITTEES.

42. *What is a committee?*

It is often convenient, if not necessary, for a deliberative body to commit, or entrust, to one or more of its members such matters as require a more extended examination, or a more free discussion, or a more elaborate preparation for action, than is compatible with the formalities essential to the government of large assemblies. The party or parties to whom such matters are committed, is called a committee.

43. *Is a matter referred to a committee for no other purpose than for those just specified?*

A matter may be referred to a committee merely as a suitable means of collecting information concerning it. Not unfrequently the reference to a committee is only a convenient mode of postponing the consideration of a subject.

44. *May a part only of a subject be referred to a committee?*

A subject may be referred to a committee, in part

in England, in the Latin form of the commission to justices of the peace. The part of the document wherein the word occurs, runs thus: "We have also assigned you, and every two or more of you, *quorum unum*, A B *vel* C D *vel* E F, &c., *esse volumus*, that is, *of whom* we will that A B or C D or E F, &c., shall be one." This made it necessary that certain individuals, who, in the language of the commission, were said to be of the "*quorum*," should be present during the transaction of business.

Hence, in legislative and other deliberative bodies, has arisen the application of the term to such a number of the members as may be declared necessary to give validity to any business proceeding.

or in whole, at the pleasure of the assembly; or different parts of the same subject may be referred to different committees.

45. *What is the differencc between a Select and a Standing Committee?*

In most deliberative assemblies, it is found advantageous to have several permanent committees, to each of which a particular subject, or class of subjects is in general referred. Such committees are called *Standing* Committees.

Now and then, however, there arises a subject not properly referable to any one of the standing committees, or, for some cause, or other, more proper to be entrusted to a committee chosen expressly for the occasion. Such a committee is called a *Select* Committee.

46. *Are committees bound by particular instructions, or left to act according to their own discretion?*

The office of a committee is essentially that of an agent, or factor; and as an agent is bound always to obey the instructions of his principal, or if under no special instructions, he is to do what best he can to promote the interest committed to his charge, so a committee is bound at all times to follow out strictly the directions given by the assembly, or if left to their own discretion, their duty is to exercise their best judgment in carrying out the will of the body for whom they act.*

* The assembly may, at any time during the progress of their deliberations, revoke instructions previously given, impose new ones producing an entirely different aspect or direction of affairs, or leave them altogether to their own discretion.

47. *How is the number of which a committee shall consist, decided upon?*

If, in the motion to appoint a committee, whether select or standing, the number of persons of which it shall consist, is not specified, it is customary for members, without resort to a motion, to propose different numbers, as each may prefer. The President, then following the rule observed in the case of filling blanks,* puts to vote the question on each number, beginning with the highest, till he comes to that on which the assembly can agree.

48. *After the number is fixed, of which a committee shall be composed, what is the mode of selecting the members of it?*

The members of a committee may be appointed by the presiding officer, either in virtue of some standing rule, or in accordance with a motion made for the occasion; or they may be elected by ballot, provided a resolution is passed to that effect; or, lastly, they may be chosen by an open nomination and vote of the assembly.

49. *In the choice of members to serve on a committee, is regard to be had to their previously known, or expressed opinions on the matters to be referred to them?*

The general rule is, that he who is known to be utterly opposed to a proposition, should not be appointed on a committee, charged merely with the amendment or modification of that proposition; since his aim would not be to amend, but to destroy.

* See page 98.

If, therefore, the design of the commitment is *amendment*, which is here taken for granted, those only ought to be members of the committee, who, though friendly to the measure, or proposition, in the main, still desire to amend, or alter it in certain particulars.

This rule, however, is rather *discretionary* than imperative; since the appointing power, whether the President or the assembly, is under no positive obligation to observe it.*

50. *Is a committce free to organize in its own way, or must it be organized under special instructions from the assembly?*

Every committee has the *right* to organize in its own way; that is, is perfectly free to appoint its own officers.† But, as in the assembly, it is usually considered polite and proper to place on the committee both the mover and the seconder of the motion to raise such committee, so in the committee itself, it is, as a matter of *courtesy*, so customary as to amount almost to a rule, to appoint the member first named, or selected, to act as its chairman, and to report its proceedings to the body at large.‡

* It is the duty of the Secretary, when a committee has been appointed, to make out a list of the members, and send it, together with a copy of the instructions under which they are to act, to the person first named on the list.

† See, however, the answer to question 68, and the note.

‡ The person first named on a committee always acts as chairman *pro. tem.* till the permanent Chairman is appointed. It is his duty, accordingly, to call a meeting of his colleagues at the earliest convenience, and so open the way to business.

51. *Is a committee at liberty to fix its own time and place of meeting?*

In respect to the time and place of meeting, as in respect to the disposition of the matters entrusted to it, a committee is always subject to the direction of the assembly; and if, when ordered to meet at a particular time, it fails of that time, it is not at liberty to enter upon duty, till again directed to sit by the assembly.

But, if left without special direction in this regard, the committee has power, as a matter of course, to choose such time and place as may be deemed expedient; provided always, the time be not that during which the assembly itself is in session.

52. *May the members of a committee transact the business referred to them, by separate consultation, and without the formality of a regular meeting?*

Nothing is the *act* of a committee, which is not done or agreed to, in the committee duly assembled, as such. There can, therefore, be no such thing as the report of a committee, made by separate consultation, and without the formality of a regular meeting of its members.

53. *Are committees never allowed to sit in deliberation, while the assembly itself is in session?*

If the business is such as to require immediate attention, or the assembly is anxious for despatch, a committee may be ordered to sit, while the body itself is in session. But, unless so ordered, it is contrary to a rule founded on obvious propriety, for a committee to sit while the assembly is sitting.*

If, therefore, the body itself, after an adjournment, is found to be in session, while the committee is yet engaged in its deliberations, it is the duty of the committee forthwith to rise and attend the assembly.

54. *Is it necessary in order to the transaction of business in committee, that all the members of the committee should be present?*

The number of members necessary to form a quorum for the transaction of business in a committee, is sometimes fixed by a vote, or by a standing rule of the assembly. Where, however, this is not the case, a majority is, in this country, commonly considered requisite to constitute a quorum, or else whatever other proportion may be necessary to a quorum in the assembly itself.

55. *What subjects are usually referred to committees, and what is the ordinary mode of proceeding in them?*

To committees, as before observed,† are usually re-

* The rule that committees are not to sit during the session of the assembly, is founded upon the principle, that the presence of the members constituting the committee, as well as that of all others, is necessary to full and efficient service in the body. The absence of a single member is often a great disadvantage.

The meetings of the assembly itself are, on this account, not unfrequently so appointed as to time, as to allow full opportunity for the discharge of duty in committees. Thus, it is well known that in Congress the daily sessions do not commence till twelve o'clock, mainly out of regard to the immense amount of labor devolving upon committees in preparing and digesting business for action in the two Houses.

† See answer to question 42.

ferred such papers, propositions, or other matters, as require to be digested, amended, or examined with a minuteness of detail very inconvenient, if not quite impracticable, in the full assembly. Accordingly, they are often obliged to make many personal inquiries, to examine lengthy documents bearing upon the subject confided to them, to examine witnesses, and otherwise to pursue protracted investigations.

In regard to the mode of proceeding in committee, the order, in most respects, is the same with that observed in the assembly itself. Thus, nothing is considered as an *act* of the committee, which has not been done in a meeting regularly convened; wherein business must be transacted by motions duly made, seconded and passed, as in the assembly.

56. *Is it necessary for a committee to append to their report a resolution respecting the subject of their deliberations, and to recommend its adoption by the assembly?*

The very object of a committee is to prepare business for the *action* of the assembly. It is, therefore, settled by an almost universal usage, that every report of a committee should conclude with a resolution.*

57. *What course is adopted in the case of breaches of order, or disorderly words in a committee?*

A breach of order in committee is not punishable by the committee itself; neither are disorderly words.

* If the committee has been raised merely to gather information, or if they should think proper to render a verbal report, declaring the matter of no sufficient interest or importance to require action, the report should close with a resolution to discharge the committee from the further consideration of the subject.

Both must be reported to the assembly; the disorderly words being written down as when occurring in the assembly itself.*

58. *When a subject is referred to a committee, is it left with them to treat it as they please?*

A committee may be instructed, or directed in relation to the subject committed to their charge, or not, at the pleasure of the assembly. But, if left without instructions as to the duties assigned them, they have the right to treat the matter entirely according to their own judgment, and to report to the assembly upon it in whatever manner they deem expedient.

59. *What is the course pursued in relation to papers before a committee?*

The course pursued in relation to papers is, in general, the same as that adopted in the assembly. The paper is first read through by the Secretary or the Chairman; then it is again read by the Chairman, by paragraphs or sections; he pausing, at proper intervals, to hear and put to the vote the amendments, if any, that may be offered by members. This being done, if the paper is one that has originated with the committee, the question is then taken upon the whole document, as amended or unamended.

If, however, the paper is not original with the committee, but is one that has been merely submitted for amendment, the question upon the adoption, or rejection of the whole is not, of course, to be taken; for that, as well as the amendment proposed by the committee, belongs ultimately to the assembly itself.

* See page 124.

60. *Suppose the committee should be opposed to the paper altogether, what is to be done?*

In the event of a committee being entirely opposed to a paper submitted for amendment, their course is to report it back to the assembly unamended, with the reasons therefor, if thought desirable, and then, not as members of the committee, but as members of the body at large, make what opposition to it they see fit.

61. *Is a committee at liberty to alter, by way of amendment, or otherwise, the subject-matter under consideration?*

No committee is allowed to alter the subject under deliberation, their duty being confined strictly to a consideration of its nature and bearings.

When the subject is referred with instructions, the instructions must, of course, be strictly obeyed.

62. *Is a committee at liberty to erase, interline, or otherwise mark over a paper under their consideration?*

A committee is, of course, at liberty to erase, interline, or otherwise mark any paper originating with themselves.

But, in the case of a paper submitted by the assembly, they have no right to mark, or deface it in any way, or for any purpose whatever. If they agree to propose amendments or alterations, these must be put on a separate piece of paper, and the places where it is proposed to insert them, designated by the proper line, page, paragraph, or section of the original document.

The committee may, however, if they please, report their amendment in the form of a new draft of the original paper, with the amendments duly made and inserted. This, in fact, where the alterations are minute or numerous, is decidedly the best way.

63. *Supposing a difference of opinion to exist among the members of a committee, have the minority a right to bring in a counter report?*

The reception of a report from the minority of a committee is conceded rather as a *favor* than as a *right.* This is done, though not strictly in order, partly out of courtesy, and partly for the sake of a more full development of the matter in dispute.*

* On the subject of *Minority Reports,* Mr. Cushing very justly says:—"The report of a committee being the conclusion which is agreed to by a majority of the members, the dissenting, or not-agreeing members, according to strict parliamentary practice, would have no other mode of bringing their views before the assembly than as individual members. Inasmuch, however, as such members may be supposed to have given the subject equal consideration with the other members of the committee, and may, therefore, be in possession of views and opinions equally worthy of the attention of the assembly, the practice has become general in the legislative assemblies of this country, to allow members in the minority to present their views and conclusions in the parliamentary form of a report, which is accordingly known by the somewhat incongruous appellation of a minority report. Any two, or more of the members may unite in such a report, or each one of them may express his views in a separate document.

"A minority report is not recognized as a report of the committee, or acted upon as such; it is received by courtesy, and allowed to accompany the report, as representing the opinions of the minority; and, in order to its being adopted by the assembly, it must be moved as an amendment to the report, when that comes to be considered."

For more on this subject, see page 116.

COMMITTEE OF THE WHOLE.

64. *What is a committee of the whole?*

A committee may consist, according to the pleasure of the assembly, of one member only, of a number of members, or of the entire body. A committee embracing the entire body, is called a committee of the *whole.*

65. *What is the use of a committee of the whole?*

There are times when it is best for the whole assembly, unfettered by certain parliamentary restraints, to deal with a subject after the manner adopted in ordinary committees. In such cases, it is usual for the body to resolve itself into a committee of the whole.

66. *What is the form employed in resolving an assembly into a committee of the whole?*

The form employed in resolving an assembly into a committee of the whole, is this: A member rises in his place, and moves, "*that the assembly do now resolve itself into a committee of the whole, to take under consideration the subject*" (whatever it is); and this being seconded, the question is put to vote by the presiding officer.

If decided in the affirmative, the President, after announcing the result, resigns the chair to whomsoever is named, or appointed to act as chairman of the committee, and then takes part, like other members, in the matters under deliberation.

67. *How is the Chairman of the committee of the whole appointed?*

Immediately after the passage of a resolution to go

into a committee of the whole, it is usual for the President of the assembly to name, or designate a member to act as chairman of the committee.

This he does either in virtue of some special rule or in accordance with established custom: if in virtue of a rule, the person so named, or designated is thereby appointed: if merely in compliance with custom, the appointment may, or may not be acquiesced in according to the will of the members.

If, therefore, on going into a committee of the whole, the presiding officer, in conformity with usage, but without the authority of a special rule, assigns to a member the chairmanship of the committee, if no one objects all is right, and the appointment is valid; but if objection be made, a chairman must be appointed by a regular vote.

68. *Is the election, in such case, to be made by a vote of the members acting in the capacity of a committee, or in that of the assembly proper?*

If, as supposed in the preceding answer, the appointment of a chairman by vote becomes necessary, it must be by a vote of the assembly as such: the presiding officer resuming the chair in order to put the question.*

* Jefferson, in his Manual (Section xii.), says, that, where the appointment is to be made by vote, committees of the whole "have a right to elect one; some member, by consent, putting the question." On this, Mr. Cushing (p. 175) says:—"The statement that, where a Chairman is to be appointed by vote, the question is to be put by some member in the committee, though laid down by Mr. Jefferson, on the authority of an old writer on parliamentary proceedings, is not sanctioned by Hatsell, or borne out by the modern practice in the British parliament."

69. *What number of members constitutes a quorum in a committee of the whole?*

Whatever number constitutes a quorum in the assembly itself, constitutes a quorum in a committee of the whole.

70. *What course is taken when no quorum is present?*

When the number present in a committee of the whole becomes less than that required to form a quorum, the committee, upon motion to that effect, must rise; in which case, the presiding officer of the assembly, whose duty is always to be present in the committee, and ready, when necessary, to resume the chair, takes his proper place, and the committee of the whole is accordingly dissolved.

71. *How is a Secretary appointed in committee of the whole?*

In committee of the whole, the Clerk or Secretary of of the assembly, or his assistant, if he has one, acts as secretary.

72. *Does he record the proceedings of the committee on the journal, or minute-book of the assembly?*

The report of the committee, that is, whatever they conclude to lay before the assembly, as the *result* of their deliberation, the Clerk, or Secretary at the proper time enters, of course, upon his record; but the proceedings in committee are not recorded in his journal.

73. *Are the proceedings in a committee of the whole different from those in the assembly itself?*

The mode of proceeding and the rules of order in a committee of the whole are not essentially different from those observed in the body itself. But, as the only object of a committee is to secure a release from certain embarrasments, necessarily existent in the conduct of the assembly proper, it follows, as a matter of course, that some differences must be made in the order of proceeding.

74. *What are the principal points in which the order of proceeding in a committee of the whole, differs from that pursued in the assembly itself?*

In the assembly, a member cannot speak more than once or twice on the same subject; in committee of the whole, he may speak as often as he pleases. In the assembly, all discussions may be suddenly arrested by the use of the previous question; in committee of the whole, the previous question can never be introduced. In the assembly, the yeas and nays may be called for, and an appeal be made from the decisions of the chair; in committee of the whole, neither a call for the yeas and nays nor an appeal from the chair is allowable. In the assembly, committees of their own number may be raised at any time; in committee of the whole, a committee of their own number, that is, a sub-committee, is inadmissible. In the assembly, any breach of order may be punished; in committee of the whole, as in other committees, the matter must be referred to the assembly. In the assembly, a motion may be made and carried to adjourn to another time and place; in committee of the whole, if, for any reason, it is thought proper to discontinue their deliberations for a time, it is necessary for some one to move that the committee rise, report progress, and ask leave to sit again.

Besides all this, greater freedom every way is allowed in committee of the whole than would be admissible in the assembly; and, moreover, the proceedings in the committee, which, though leading to *results* however useful, are themselves often tedious and informal, are not required to be placed upon the record, as would be the case were they the transactions of the assembly as such.

75. *What form is observed, when the committee rise and report?*

If the motion to rise is carried, the Chairman of the committee immediately yields the chair to the President of the assembly. Then, taking his proper place among the members, he rises and informs the president that the committee of the whole have, in obedience to the order of the assembly, had the subject of (whatever it may be) under consideration; that some progress had been made in the disposition of it; and that, for want of time (or whatever other cause), having been obliged to discontinue their deliberations, they had instructed him to ask leave for the committee to sit again.

76. *If leave be granted for the committee to sit again, is it necessary for the assembly, at the time appointed,*

again formally to resolve itself into a committee of the whole?

If the motion to grant the request of the committee for another sitting be decided in the affirmative, the assembly must then also, by motion, name the time for that sitting, and, when that time arrives, it is necessary to go again regularly through the formality of resolving the assembly into a committee of the whole.

77. *What course is taken in committee of the whole, when the business referred to them, is finished?*

When the business referred to the committee of the whole, is finished, some one moves that the committee do now rise and report. This motion being passed, the President of the assembly resumes the chair, and the Chairman of the committee rising in his place among the members, states that the committee of the whole, having finished the business entrusted to them, have directed him to present a report, which is ready, whenever it is the pleasure of the assembly to receive it.

The proper way then, is to fix by motion the time for receiving the report. But often, in the matter of receiving a report, a formal motion is omitted: the assembly, if that be their pleasure, crying out, "Now! Now!" or if another time, "Monday! Tuesday!" or whatever other day they choose.

SECTION V.

PRIVILEGED QUESTIONS.

78. *What are privileged questions?*

The general rule, in deliberative bodies, is, that the question first moved and seconded, shall first be put to the vote. Circumstances, however, sometimes require a departure from this rule.

There are, accordingly, certain motions, or questions which are allowed to supersede a proposition already under debate, and which, for that reason, are denominated *privileged* questions. The question superseded, in such case, is called the *main*, or *principal* question.

79. *What are the particular circumstances that call for the use of privileged questions?*

The circumstances requiring resort to the use of privileged questions, are various. Thus, the assembly, exhausted by long-continued attention to duty, may desire to adjourn; hence the motion to adjourn is a privileged one. They may be willing longer to entertain a proposition, but not at the present time; thence arises the necessity of a motion to lie on the table. They may deem it expedient to suppress further debate on a subject; for which purpose recourse is had to what is called the previous question. They may want time for reflection, or to gather information; this creates the occasion for a motion to postpone to a certain day. They may wish to have the proposition modified or altered, or the subject investigated, to an extent or in a manner incompatible with the formalities proper to the proceedings of the full assembly; thence comes the need of a motion to commit, that is, to refer the matter to a committee. They may be favorable to a proposition in the main, but dissatisfied with certain particulars, capable of easy alteration in the assembly; that gives rise to a motion to amend. They may be anxious to get rid of a proposition altogether, and yet not to do so in a rude or indelicate manner; that is accomplished by the use of a motion to postpone indefinitely. They may have previously ordered, or appointed certain business for certain times, and the hour having arrived for such business, there may be need of a motion to proceed to the orders of the day. They may have already decided a question, and, upon further reflection, concluded to retrace their steps, and bring the matter again under deliberation; in which event, there is need of a motion to reconsider.

But there are other motions still, which circumstances require to take precedence over a question already before the assembly. These are such as arise incidentally, and, being incidental to motions of every kind, they are allowed, for the time being, to supersede the proposition under discussion, whether it be a privileged one or not. The incidental questions are such as respect the privilege of the members of the assembly, or of the whole assembly taken collectively; such as have regard to questions of order, to the reading of papers relating to the matter under debate, to the withdrawal of motions, to the suspension of rules, and the amendment of amendments.

The following is a list of all the above-mentioned questions, or motions, being here included under the general head of

PRIVILEGED QUESTIONS.*

1. Motions to adjourn.
2. Motions to lie on the table.
3. Motions for the previous question.
4. Motions to postpone to a day certain.
5. Motions to commit.
6. Motions to amend.
7. Motions to postpone indefinitely.
8. Motions for the orders of the day.
9. Motions concerning questions of privilege.
10. Motions concerning questions of order.
11. Motions for the reading of papers.
12. Motions for the withdrawal of motions.
13. Motions for the suspension of rules.
14. Motions to reconsider.

* The questions included in the list above, excepting the last, are divided by Mr. Cushing into three classes, and arranged thus:

PRIVILEGED QUESTIONS:—*Adjournment, Questions of Privilege and Orders of the Day.*

INCIDENTAL QUESTIONS:—*Questions of Order, Reading of Papers, Withdrawal of a Motion, Suspension of a Rule and Amendment of Amendments.*

SUBSIDIARY QUESTIONS:—*Lie on the Table, Previous Question, Postponement, Commitment and Amendment.*

80. *Have these privileged questions any privilege among themselves?*

The questions which thus have a right to take precedence of the main, or principal question, have, also, a certain order of precedence among themselves. In some deliberative bodies, that order is settled by a formal rule. Thus, in the 11th Rule of the United States Senate, we read:

"When a question is under debate, no motion shall be received but *to adjourn, to lie on the table, to postpone indefinitely, to postpone to a day certain, to commit, or to amend;* which several motions shall have precedence in the order they stand arranged, and the motion for adjournment shall always be in order, and be decided without debate."

The order prescribed in the 46th Rule of the House of Representatives, is the following:

"When a question is under debate, no motion shall be received, but *to adjourn, to lie on the table, for the previous question, to postpone to a day certain, to commit or amend, to postpone indefinitely;* which several motions shall have precedence in the order in which they are arranged; and no motion to postpone to a day certain, to commit, or to postpone indefinitely, being decided, shall be again allowed on the same day, and at the same stage of the bill or proposition. A motion to strike out the enacting words of a bill shall have precedence of a motion to amend, and, if carried, shall be considered equivalent to its rejection."

THE MOTION TO ADJOURN.

81. *When is a motion to adjourn in order?*

A motion to adjourn, as stated in the Senate Rule, is always in order, and, therefore, takes precedence of all others.* It must, moreover, be put without debate.

82. *Why should a motion to adjourn have precedence of all others?*

Because otherwise the body might be kept in session against its will, and that for an indefinite period of time.

83. *Must the motion to adjourn, then, be always entertained without respect to time or circumstances?*

In a general sense, a motion to adjourn may be, and usually is, said to be *always* in order. But this must be taken with some limitations. Thus, it cannot be received while a member is speaking, unless he consents to give way for that purpose; it cannot be entertained while a vote, or the process of calling the *yeas* and *nays*, is in progress; it cannot, after being once negatived, be renewed previous to the intervention of some other business; and, lastly, it must be a motion to adjourn simply, without specification of any kind; that is, merely that the assembly "*do now adjourn.*"†

* By the 48th Rule of the United States House of Representatives, not only a motion to adjourn, but also a motion to fix the day to which the House *will* adjourn, is declared to be always in order.

Under this Rule, also, a motion to fix the day, to which the House shall adjourn, is made to take precedence of a simple motion to adjourn.

† See, however, the 48th Rule of the United States House of Representatives, referred to in the preceding note.

84. *Is a motion to adjourn susceptible of amendment?*

A motion to adjourn cannot be amended; for the amendment itself would introduce new business not entitled to take precedence of the main question.

If, however, a motion to adjourn is offered, when no other proposition is before the assembly, it may be amended like any other motion.

85. *If the motion to adjourn must be made without specification of time, how is the assembly to be governed, as to the time of the next meeting?*

When a motion simply to adjourn is decided in the affirmative, the body is thereby adjourned to the next regular time of sitting; or to such time, if any, as has been appointed by previous resolution.

86. *What difference, if any, is there between a motion simply to adjourn, and a motion to adjourn sine die?*

Sine die means *without day;* that is, without a day appointed for another meeting. In reality, therefore, a motion simply to adjourn, and a motion to adjourn *sine die,* are things identical. But the form to adjourn *sine die* is mainly employed in relation to bodies, whereof no re-assembling is contemplated; in which case, of course, to adjourn *sine die* is the same as to *dissolve* the assembly altogether.

87. *What formality, if any, on the part of the presiding officer, is necessary to give efficacy to a motion to adjourn?*

Though a resolution to adjourn has been duly passed,

there is, nevertheless, properly no adjournment, until the President has officially announced the same from the chair.

88. *What becomes of a proposition which has been arrested, while under debate, by a vote for adjournment?*

When a proposition has been interrupted in its course by a motion to adjourn, it is thereby removed from the body, and, if again brought up, must be introduced in the usual way.

THE MOTION TO LIE ON THE TABLE.

89. *When is a motion to lie on the table employed?*

It sometimes happens while one matter is under deliberation, another claims the immediate attention of the assembly; or for some other reason, it is deemed expedient, for the time being, to discontinue the discussion of a pending proposition, with a view to take up the subject at a more convenient season. In such case a motion is made to lay the subject on the table, that is, to lay it aside, till it is the pleasure of the body to resume the consideration of it.

90. *What rank does it hold among privileged questions?*

A motion to lie on the table usually takes precedence of all motions, except the motion to adjourn, a question of privilege, and a motion for the orders of the day.*

* In Congress the motion to lie on the table supersedes all motions, except a motion to adjourn. See Rules of the Senate and House, page 76.

91. *Is the motion to lie on the table debatable?*

The motion to lie on the table can neither be debated nor amended. It is, therefore, often employed to get rid of a question altogether.

92. *What is the effect of this motion, if decided affirmatively?*

The effect of a motion to lie on the table, if decided in the affirmative, is to withdraw from the assembly the main question, together with all other secondary, or incidental questions relating thereto, until, by motion duly made and passed, it be the pleasure of the body to resume the consideration thereof.

93. *What if it be decided negatively?*

A motion to lie on the table, when decided by a negative vote, leaves the pending question wholly untouched, and its discussion is, therefore, immediately resumed, and continued just as though no interruption had taken place.

THE PREVIOUS QUESTION.

94. *What is the previous question?*

Whenever it is thought desirable suddenly to arrest discussion, and test immediately the sense of an assembly, in respect to a subject under debate, there is a motion, or question expressly for this purpose, which is denominated "THE PREVIOUS QUESTION."

95. *What was the origin and design of this motion?*

This motion was introduced, in 1604, by Sir Harry

Vane, in the British House of Commons, and was designed to suppress motions which, if publicly discussed, might bring censure upon the government, or upon individuals occupying high official station.

96. *What was its form and effect?*

The original form of the previous question was,—"*Shall the main question be put?*" This was simply asking whether, after the debate was over, however long or earnest it might be, the main question should ultimately be put to the vote. If decided in the affirmative, of course, the discussion might be resumed, and continued, till the subject was regularly and finally disposed of.

In the event of a negative decision, however, which was precisely the object sought by the mover, all discussion of the main question was at an end, and more than that, the whole subject was taken from before the House for the remainder of the session. This was a natural result; for what would be the use of continuing to discuss a question which the House had already determined, should not (after all) be put to the vote?

When afterwards the form of the previous question was changed to that which it now has, which is. "*Shall the main question be now put?*" an affirmative decision entirely precluded all further debate on the main, or principal question, and brought the subject immediately to the test of a vote; while a negative decision, though operating still in the suppression of debate, did not necessarily remove the main question from before the House for the whole session, but for the rest of the day only; so that it might be renewed, if thought desirable, on the next, or on some succeeding day. This is the present operation of the previous question in the British Parliament.

In this country, an affirmative decision of the previous question has the same effect precisely, as it has in England, that is, it brings the main question, without further delay or debate, directly to a vote. And in such case, the pending amendments, if any, are first, in their order, put to vote, and then, of course, forthwith the main question.* But a negative decision of it operates differently; for that assumes, that, if the main question is not now to be put, (which is what a negative decision declares,) then that question is still subject to debate, just as it would have been, had the previous question never been demanded or applied.

97. *Is this the effect of a negative decision in all deliberative bodies?*

In the House of Representatives of the United States, its effect is to suppress the main question for the rest of the day only, just as in the British Parliament. In the House of Representatives of Massachusetts, and in the House of Assembly of New York, the effect of a negative decision of the previous question is to leave the main question with all pending amendments just where it was; that is, under debate, till disposed of in

* Formerly in the House of Representatives, the previous question, if decided in the affirmative, brought the House immediately to a vote on the main question, to the exclusion of all amendments and incidental motions. This was changed (Jan. 14, 1840,) and the present order, namely, that indicated in the text above, was established.

the usual way. And, in all deliberative assemblies in this country, it is usually taken for granted, unless otherwise ordered by a special rule, that a negative decision of the previous question leaves the main question and all amendments thereto, under deliberation just as it found them.

98. *Why is this motion sometimes called the "gag-law"?*

Since the effect of an affirmative decision of the previous question is to preclude all further debate, and bring the main question directly to a vote, it is in this country employed almost exclusively for the purpose of arresting unprofitable discussion, and so hastening a decision.

It is easy, however, to make an abusive application of the previous question, by rendering it subservient to the purpose of cutting off the most wholesome and necessary discussions, and so compelling members to be silent, who ought for the sake of truth and justice to be heard. Hence Mr. Jefferson has said: "Therefore, it ought not to be favored, but restricted within as narrow limits as possible." This unjust use of the previous question is what has often secured to it the appellation of the "*gag-law.*"

99. *Can a motion so important as this, and so liable to be abused, be entertained upon its being offered by one member only, and seconded by another, as is the case with most other questions?*

In the British Parliament any member may move the previous question, and, if seconded by another, it is thereby put into requisition. This is done also, in many assemblies in this country.

In the House of Representatives, however, it can only be admitted, when demanded by a majority of the members present.* When first recognized by the House, (April 7th, 1789) it could be introduced by a call from *five members*. It was afterwards (Dec. 23d, 1811) resolved, as in the case of a call for the yeas and nays, that *one-fifth of the members present*, should be necessary to a call for the previous question. This continued to be the Rule till February 24th, 1840. At that time a change was made, by which, as stated above, the previous question can be admitted, only when demanded by a majority of the members present.†

100. *How does the previous question rank among privileged questions?*

The previous question has the same rank as the motion to postpone, the motion to commit, and the motion to amend. It cannot, therefore, if first put, be superseded by any one of these.

It yields the precedence, however, to a motion to adjourn, to lie on the table, to a motion respecting the rights and privileges of the members, or of the assembly at large, or to a motion for the orders of the day.

* That the use of the previous question ought to be under some limitation greater than that which is customary in the case of other motions, seems very obvious. In all deliberative bodies, therefore, the number, at whose call it may be admitted, ought to be fixed by a special rule.

† See Rules of Order for the House of Representatives, No. 50.

101. *Is a motion for the previous question debatable?*

No debate is allowable on a motion for the previous question. Neither is it susceptible of amendment. All questions of order, moreover, arising incidentally thereon, must be decided without discussion, whether appeal be had from the chair or not.

THE MOTION TO POSTPONE.

102. *What is the object of a motion to postpone?*

The object of a motion to postpone is, either to defer the consideration of a pending proposition till a more convenient season, or to get rid of it altogether without coming directly to a vote upon it. The motion to postpone, therefore, is, according to the aim of the mover, either for a specified time, or for a period indefinite.

103. *What rank among privileged questions does a motion to postpone hold?*

The motion to postpone holds the same rank with the previous question, the motion to commit, and the motion to amend, and cannot by any of these be superseded. If, however, the motion to postpone be put, and lost, the pending proposition is nevertheless subject to the application of the co-ordinate motions; that is, the previous question, the motion to commit, and the motion to amend.

104. *What becomes of a proposition which has been interrupted by the passage of a motion to postpone?*

A proposition thus interrupted by the motion to

postpone is thereby removed from before the assembly, together with all matters pertaining to it.

105. *Can a motion to postpone be amended?*

If a motion is offered to postpone to a day certain, that is, to a specified time, it may be amended by substituting a different time. The time, in such case, however, may be regarded as a blank, to be filled in the manner described on page 98 following.

106. *What is the aim of a motion for indefinite postponement?*

The aim of a motion to postpone indefinitely, is to get rid of a proposition altogether without coming directly to a vote upon it; for, when decided affirmatively, the effect is to quash the proposition entirely.

107. *Can a motion to postpone indefinitely be debated, or amended?*

A motion for the indefinite postponement of a subject is generally held to be incapable, either of debate, or amendment.*

108. *What is the effect upon the pending proposition, if a motion to postpone is decided in the negative?*

A negative decision of a motion to postpone has no

* Cushing (Manual, page 96) however, says,—"If a motion is made for an indefinite postponement, it may be moved to amend the motion, by making it to a day certain. If any other day is desired, it may be moved as an amendment to the amendment; or it may be moved as an independent motion, when the amendment has been rejected."

effect whatever upon the pending proposition; which is then to be treated in all respects as if no such motion had been made.

THE MOTION TO COMMIT.

109. *When is a motion to commit employed?*

When the matter of a proposition is such, in general, as the assembly can approve, while the form, in which it comes, is so objectionable, that it would be inconvenient to give it the required shape in the assembly itself, it is usual to refer the subject to a committee.

If there be a standing committee within whose province the subject would properly fall, the matter goes properly to that committee; if not, a select committee is raised for that purpose.

110. *In the event of there being such a standing committee, must the matter be referred to that committee?*

The assembly may, if for any reason it be thought best, raise a select committee for any given subject, though there be, already existing, a standing committee, to whom the subject should otherwise be referred.

But, if it be doubtful whether a particular standing committee is the one that ought to have charge of the matter, and some members are found proposing a reference to the standing, while others prefer to give the subject to a select committee, the motion to refer to the standing committee should be first submitted to a vote of the assembly.

111. *Is a motion to commit subject to amendment?*

A motion to commit may be amended variously. It may be amended by substituting one committee, or kind of committee for another; by increasing, or lessening the number of members proposed; or by adding directions, or instructions in regard to the subject committed.

112. *What is the rank of a motion to commit among privileged questions?*

The motion to commit is in the same rank as the previous question and the motion to postpone, and cannot, therefore, be superseded by either of them.

It, however, has the precedence over a motion to amend.

113. *What is the effect of an affirmative decision of a motion to commit?*

An affirmative decision of a motion to commit takes the subject of course from before the assembly; if decided negatively, however, the subject remains before the assembly, and may then, if desirable, be subjected to the operation of the previous question, the motion to postpone, or to amend.

MOTIONS TO AMEND.

114. *What is a motion to amend?*

When a proposition is in *substance* agreeable to the wishes of an assembly, but in *form*, or in some of its *details* objectionable, it is customary, by motions to that effect, to correct, curtail, enlarge, or otherwise modify it according to the will of the body. Motions for this purpose are called motions to amend.

115. *Is it within the province of a deliberative body thus to alter the character of a proposition submitted for their decision?*

The primary and legitimate use of a motion to amend, as the term implies, is so to correct, or improve the form, or statement of a proposition, as to aid it in reaching the object which it aims to accomplish. A motion to amend, therefore, is properly an act friendly to the proposition to be amended.

But a proposition once moved, seconded, and stated from the chair, is then the property of the assembly, and there is nothing to hinder the introduction of motions to alter it in any way whatever.

It is, therefore, perfectly competent for the assembly whenever they think proper, either so to amend a proposition, as to make it more truly answerable to its object, or altogether to turn it away from its original purpose, and render it subservient to objects entirely different and adverse. Accordingly, a proposition is not unfrequently so altered by what are called motions to amend, that its original friends and movers are compelled finally to vote against it in its amended shape. Thus, motions to amend are sometimes made to work the defeat of a proposition, and are, in fact, often employed for this express purpose.

So entire is the change often effected under color of amendment, that, where no special rule exists to the contrary, matters utterly incompatible with the proposition under consideration, are engrossed upon it, and, in some cases, everything of the original motion, after the initiatory words, "*Resolved that,*" is struck out, and a proposition entirely different added.

116. *May an assembly then fix, by special rule, the limits within which an amendment shall be allowed to operate?*

In order to prevent the improper use of motions to amend, some deliberative bodies have established rules on the subject. Thus, the rule in the United States House of Representatives is, that "no motion, or proposition on a subject different from that under consideration shall be admitted under color of an amendment. No bill, or resolution shall at any time be amended by annexing thereto, or incorporating therewith, any other bill or resolution pending before the House.*

This, or some similar restriction, seems highly needful, and ought everywhere to be adopted as a rule.

117. *In what way are amendments usually made?*

Amendments, whether applied to original motions, or to other amendments, are usually effected in one of these three ways: (1) by the insertion or addition of words or sentences; (2) by the removal or striking out of words and sentences; or (3) by the striking out of some words or sentences, and the insertion of others in their stead.

* See Jefferson's Manual, page 145; also, Cushing's Manual, page 324.

118. *What is the proper order of proceeding in making amendments in these several ways?*

When a proposition consists of several parts, paragraphs, or sections, or is expressed in a series of resolutions, the proper order of proceeding is to begin with the first, and amend, if necessary, each of the parts, paragraphs, sections, or resolutions in order.

119. *Is it in order to make amendments to amendments, and, if so, to what extent can this process be carried?*

It is quite in order to amend an amendment; but here the process must terminate, an amendment of an amendment to an amendment being wholly inadmissible.

120. *Why is such an amendment not allowed?*

Were amendments heaped upon amendments in this way, the result would be not a facilitating of the business of the assembly, but a very serious embarrassment. Hence, by a well settled usage, the process of amending is forbidden to go beyond an amendment to an amendment.

121. *But suppose the object sought in a motion to amend an amendment to an amendment, be a desirable one, how, since such a motion is inadmissible, can that object be reached by the assembly?*

Whenever an amendment to an amendment seems itself to require amendment, since this is not allowed to be done by a regular motion to that effect, the object desired can, nevertheless, be easily obtained, by first rejecting the amendment to the amendment, and then, after amending it in the manner required, offering it again in its altered form as an amendment to the first amendment, which is, of course, entirely in order.*

122. *Is it in order to alter, or amend what has already been agreed to by the assembly?*

If the assembly has already, by vote, agreed, either to receive, or to reject a proposed amendment, that which has thus been agreed to, cannot be altered, or amended. Thus, if it has been voted to receive as an amendment a given clause, or paragraph, it is not in order thereafter to amend this amendment; and, if it has been agreed in the like manner, *not* to strike out certain words, those words cannot afterwards be amended: the vote *not* to strike out being in effect a vote to *retain* them, as they stand.

Neither can that which has once been disapproved by a vote of the body, be again moved in that form as an amendment.

123. *Is there, then, no way of removing, or inserting, as the case may be, words or paragraphs which it has once been decided by vote to retain, or reject?*

If an amendment which proposes to strike out a par-

* "Thus," says Cushing, in illustration of this, "if a proposition consist of A B, and it is proposed to amend by inserting C D, it may be moved to amend the amendment by inserting E F; but it cannot be moved to amend this amendment, as for example, by inserting G. The only mode by which this can be reached, is to reject the amendment in the form in which it is presented, namely, to insert E F, and to move it in the form in which it is desired to be amended, namely, to insert E G F."

ticular clause, or paragraph is once rejected, a motion simply to strike out the same words, or part of them, is not in order; but a motion to strike out the same words, or a part of them, in connection with other words *is* in order; "provided always, the coherence to be struck out be so substantial, as to make this effectually a different proposition."*

If, on the other hand, an amendment which proposes to strike out, be agreed to, it is not allowable to move to insert the same words, or part of them; but it is quite in order to move to insert the same, or part of the same words in connection with others; provided, as before, the coherence to be inserted form, in effect, a different proposition.

124. *When it is proposed to amend by striking out certain words, and inserting others in their stead, would it be in order to move for the striking out and the insertion separately?*

The motion to strike out one thing, and insert another in its place, is in reality a double motion. It may, therefore, at the pleasure of the assembly, or even at the call of a single member, be divided. In that case the question is first taken on the striking out, and (that being decided in the affirmative) it is then taken on the insertion. In the event of a negative decision of the motion to strike out, the motion to insert does not of course follow.

125. *When the motion to amend by striking out one thing, and inserting another in its place, is once put and*

* Jefferson's Manual, sec. 35.

lost in the undivided, or double form, can the same motion be renewed?

No motion to amend, whether to strike out, to insert, or to strike out *and* insert, when once lost, can again be moved in the same form.*

126. *Is it in order to propose an amendment which is inconsistent with an amendment already adopted?*

An amendment which is in conflict with one already accepted, is certainly out of order, and ought at once to be rejected.

127. *Is it not the duty of the presiding officer in such case to reject, or suppress, such an amendment, if proposed?*

Though an amendment that is incompatible with one already approved by the assembly, offers, by that very circumstance, a fit ground for its rejection by the assembly, it is not competent for the presiding officer to suppress it, as being contrary to order; for, were he allowed to bring questions of consistency like this within the circle of the rules of order, he might often usurp a negative on important modifications, and defeat instead of subserving the will of the assembly.

128. *What is the proper mode of stating a motion to amend?*

The proper mode of stating a proposition to amend, is first to read the whole passage to be amended,—then the words proposed to be struck out, or the words pro-

* See answers to questions 122 and 123.

posed to be inserted, or the words proposed to be struck out and those offered as a substitute, as the case may be,—and, last of all, the whole passage as it will stand when amended.

129. *In what particular order, if any, must amendments be put to the vote?*

An amendment must, of course, come to the vote before the main question, and, in like manner, an amendment to an amendment must take the precedence. But, in the event of there being several proposed amendments to an amendment, they should be put to the vote in the order in which they are moved; not however, because of any established order of precedence, but in view of the fitness, or propriety of the thing.

130. *What is the proper form of the question on a motion to strike out?*

The form in Parliament always is,—shall the words proposed to be struck out stand as part of the principal question: the question being not, *Shall they be struck out*, but *Shall they stand?*

But in this country, the form of the question always is,—Shall the words be *stricken out?**

131. *What rank among privileged questions is held by a motion to amend?*

A motion to amend holds the same rank with the previous question, and indefinite postponement; consequently, that which is first moved must be first put.

* See Jefferson's Manual, sec. 35, and Cushing, p. 67.

132. *By what motions is the motion to amend liable to be superseded?*

The motion to amend is liable to be superseded by a motion to postpone to a day certain, that is, to a particular time; so that amendment and postponement being in competition, the motion to postpone takes precedence.

A motion to amend may also be superseded by a motion to commit; so that the latter motion being offered while an amendment is under discussion, it must be put to the vote first.

DIVISION OF A QUESTION.

133. *What other changes, if any, in the nature of amendments, can be wrought, by motion, upon propositions before a deliberative assembly?*

There are several other changes which may be comprehended under the general name of amendments, to which a proposition under discussion may be subjected. Thus, it may be expedient to divide a question, or to effect an addition, or union of several propositions, or to transpose the different parts of a proposition, or to fill up blanks designedly left for the action of the assembly.

134. *What do you mean by dividing a question?*

When a motion embraces several parts, each of which forms substantially a separate proposition, the resolution of it into distinct motions, or questions is called dividing the question.

135. *What advantage is there in such a division of the question, and how is it effected?*

A motion may, in the form of a single proposition, comprehend in reality two or more propositions, one or more of which alone might be acceptable to the assembly, while the rest might be decidedly objectionable.

The advantage, therefore, of a division of the question is, that it affords the assembly an opportunity to receive, or to reject what part it thinks proper, and that, without embarrassment. The division of a question is effected by an order of the assembly, obtained upon motion introduced in the usual way; and when divided, the several divisions, or proposition, into which it has been resolved, must be voted upon and decided in the order in which they stand.

136. *What should be the character of a motion to divide a question?*

A motion to divide a question should state particularly the manner, in which it proposed to make the division.

137. *Is a motion for a division of the question, itself capable of alteration, or amendment?*

A motion to divide is subject to precisely the same rules of amendment as any other.

138. *Is it competent for any member that thinks proper to require a division of the question?*

It is not unfrequently claimed that any member has a right to demand the division of a question, and that without a vote of the assembly. But for this claim there is no good foundation, unless, as is sometimes the case, there is a standing rule in the body to that effect. "The fact is," (Jef. Man., Sect. xxxvi.) "that the only mode of separating a complicated question is by moving amendments to it;" or by an order of the assembly obtained, as before said, upon motion introduced, and carried in the usual way.

139. *Under what circumstances is an addition, or union of the parts of a question, expedient?*

Whenever, as often occurs, a motion embraces in *form* two propositions, while in *substance* there really exists but one, it is usually thought expedient to add or unite the separate propositions, so as to present the whole matter to the assembly as a single question.

140. *What is the mode of proceeding in order to effect such addition, or union?*

The addition, or union may be effected, either by voting down one of the propositions, and then incorporating its substance with the other, or by referring the whole matter to a committee, with instructions to put the two propositions in the form of a single question, or motion.

141. *What is the process in the case of transposition?*

Whenever it is deemed expedient to transpose a clause, paragraph, or section, there should be a motion to remove it from the place where it is, and another to insert it in the place preferred.

THE FILLING OF BLANKS.

142. *What is the order, or process observed in filling blanks?*

When blanks for the insertion of particular times or numbers are designedly left in a proposition to be filled by a vote of the asssembly, the motions to fill such blanks are dealt with, not as amendments, but as original motions, and must be decided upon before putting the main question.

In the event of there being several different propositions respecting the times or numbers proper to fill the blanks, the general rule is, to put the question first on the *longest time* and the *largest sum.* In the British House of Commons, however the rule is that the question shall be put first on the *smallest* sum, and the *longest* time.*

ORDERS OF THE DAY.

143. *What is meant by the orders of the day?*

It is often expedient to order, by resolution, a particular subject to be brought up for consideration on a particular day. Subjects thus ordered, or appointed for a specified time, are called the orders of the day for that particular day.

* The rule laid down in Jefferson's Manual, and that which generally prevails where there is no special rule to the contrary, is thus expressed (in Section xxxiii): "In all cases of time or number, we must consider whether the larger comprehends the lesser, as in a question to what day a postponement shall be, the number of a committee, amount of a fine, term of an imprisonment, term of irredeemability of a loan, or the *terminus in quem* (*limit to which*) in any other case. Then the question must begin *à maximo* (*from the greatest*). Or whether the lesser includes the greater, as in questions on the limitation of the rate of interest, on what day the session shall be closed by adjournment, on what day the next shall commence, when an act shall commence, or the *terminus à quo* (*the limit from which*) in any other case, where the question must begin *à minimo* (*from the least*). The object being not to begin at that extreme which and more being within every man's wish, no one could negative it, and yet if we should vote in the affirmative, every question for more would be precluded; but at that extreme which would unite few, and then advance or recede till you get to a number which will unite a bare majority."

144. *When a question is thus assigned for a given day, is it necessary to specify the particular hour of the day?*

If no particular hour of the day is specified, the order, or subject appointed, may claim, and is entitled to the entire day. If, however, a particular time of the day *is* named, the order of the day cannot be made a privileged question; that is, cannot supersede any pending question, till the appointed hour arrrives.

145. *What is the rank of a motion for the orders of the day?*

A motion for the orders of the day commonly takes precedence of all other business, except a motion to adjourn, or a question of privilege.

146. *Supposing several orders, or subjects to have been assigned for the same day, can the motion for the orders of the day be used to call up one of them in particular to the exclusion of the rest?*

It cannot; the motions must be for *the orders* of the day collectively.

147. *How, then, in case of dispute, can it be decided which shall be acted upon first?*

The rule established by custom is, that they shall be taken up in the order, in which they stand on the record.

148. *Suppose, of several orders appointed for the same day, one only is assigned for a particular hour, can the rest, in the event of their being time sufficient, be acted upon before that hour?*

If, among several orders of the day, one is named for

a particular hour, the rest may be acted on in due succession, as they stand upon the record, till that hour arrives; when the subject appropriate to it must come up next in order.

149. *Suppose that none of the orders are taken up before the hour fixed upon for that particular one, what course is then pursued?*

The order for that particular hour is first considered, and the rest follow as they stand on the record.

150. *Suppose the motion for the orders of the day be decided in the negative, what then is the course to be taken?*

In the event of a motion for the orders of the day being decided in the negative, the pending question is thereby entitled to be first considered, and decided upon.

151. *Can a motion for the orders of the day be made, while a member is speaking?*

A motion for the orders of the day cannot be made, while a member is speaking, because it is a breach of order to interrupt him, while speaking, unless by a call to order.

152. *What becomes of a question, or proposition which has been superseded by a motion for the orders of the day?*

A question superseded by a motion for the orders of the day, is removed entirely from before the assembly, and, if renewed, must be brought up *de novo* in the ordinary way.

153. *In the event of an omission to act upon the orders of the day on the day appointed, what becomes of them?*

Orders of the day, if not acted upon on the day appointed for them, are thereby made of no effect; that is, they cannot, unless renewed for some other day, be regarded in the light of privileged questions.

But, in case of a special rule or by-law to that effect, orders for a given day, when not disposed of on the day appointed, may have precedence on every day thereafter, till finally decided upon.

154. *Can orders of the day, when once made and appointed, be discharged?*

Orders of the day may be discharged at any time, and a new order made for a different day.

QUESTIONS OF PRIVILEGE.

155. *What are questions of privilege?*

Questions of privilege are those that involve the rights and privileges of individual members, or of the whole body taken collectively: as where a dispute arises respecting the presence of persons not belonging to the body, or where a quarrel takes place between members themselves.

156. *What rank does a question of privilege hold among privileged questions?*

A question of privilege prevails for the time, over all other propositions, except a motion to adjourn.

157. *What becomes of a proposition that has been superseded by a question of privilege?*

A proposition superseded by a question of privilege, is regarded as still pending, and must be taken up again just where it was left off.

QUESTIONS OF ORDER.

158. *What are questions of order?*

It is the right and the duty of every member of a deliberative assembly to see, as far as may be, that the rules of order, in every proceeding, be duly observed. He may, therefore, and should in all cases of a breach of the rules, rise to the point of order, and insist upon its being duly enforced.

But, if in a case of this kind, a difference of opinion exists, as to whether a rule *has* been violated or not, the question, which is thence called a question of order, must be determined before the application of the rule can be insisted upon.

159. *But how is it to be determined?*

A question of order is usually settled by the decision of the chair and without debate. If, however, the decision of the president be deemed unsatisfactory, it is competent for any member to *appeal* from that decision, and demand a vote of the house on the matter.

On an appeal, the question is stated by the presiding officer, and usually in this form: "*Shall the decision of the chair be sustained?*" or, "*Shall the decision of the chair stand as the decision of the assembly?*"

160. *Is a motion on an appeal, like this, debatable?*

A motion on an appeal from the decision of the chair is to be debated, and in all respects treated like any other question; and, what is altogether against order in other cases, the presiding officer is permitted to participate in the debate.

161. *What effect, if any, beyond the mere delay, is produced upon a pending proposition by the introduction of a question of order?*

It sometimes happens, that the decision of a question of order disposes of the question out of which it arose; but, with this exception, a pending proposition remains wholly unaffected by the introduction and decision of a question of order, and the consideration of it is to be resumed just at the point, where it was interrupted.

MOTIONS FOR THE READING OF PAPERS.

162. *When, if not always, is it necessary to introduce a motion for the reading of papers?*

When papers, or documents of any kind are laid before a deliberative assembly, every member has a right to have them read once before he can be required to vote upon them.

Accordingly, when the reading of a paper which has immediate reference to the matter under discussion is called for, the paper is of course read by the clerk, or secretary, without the formality of a vote to that effect.

163. *Has, then, any member, the right at any time, to call for the reading of any paper that he may deem pertinent to the matter under debate?*

No member has a right to read or have read any book, paper, or other document, which is not obviously essential to a right understanding of the question before the house. This is manifestly a very proper limitation; for without it, such delay and embarrassment would often ensue as to prevent the transaction of the most important business.

When, therefore, a member desires to read or have read a paper that seems to transcend the limits within which such reading ought to be confined, even though it should be his own previously prepared speech on the subject, he must, for this purpose, if any one objects, obtain permission so to do by a vote of the assembly.

164. *Is the reading of a paper ordinarily objected to in an assembly?*

That depends upon its apparent aim, or obvious tendency. If the aim clearly is to shed light upon the subject, and so conduce to a more intelligent disposition of it, the paper is ordinarily read, under the direction of the presiding officer, without the least objection. But, when the purpose of the proposed reading is obviously to create delay, or where, for any reason, it seems likely to operate as an abuse of the time and patience of the assembly, it is generally met with a most decided negative.

MOTIONS FOR THE WITHDRAWAL OF MOTION.

165. *When is it necessary to offer a motion for the withdrawal of a motion?*

When a motion is once moved, seconded, and stated from the chair, it is thereafter the property of the house, and cannot be withdrawn by the mover.*

If, however, the mover, either for the purpose of modifying it, or substituting another in its place, or for any other purpose, desires to withdraw it from the House, he is not at liberty so to do, without leave obtained by a motion to that effect, regularly made and passed in the usual way. If the motion for a withdrawal is negatived, the matter must be treated just as if no motion to withdraw had been proposed.

MOTIONS FOR THE SUSPENSION OF RULES.

166. *When is a motion for the suspension of a rule necessary?*

When anything is proposed which is forbidden by a special rule, but which is deemed to be of such importance as to warrant a suspension of that rule, it is necessary to make a motion to that effect. Of course, the motion to suspend precedes the original motion.

* This is the rule in Parliament, and the general rule in the Legislative bodies of this country. There are, however, exceptions to it; as in the state Legislature of Pennsylvania; where a motion, or resolution may be withdrawn by the mover at any time previous to an amendment, or a final decision.

167. *Can a motion to suspend the operation of a special rule, be carried by the will of a bare majority?*

If there be no standing-rule, or by-law to the contrary, a motion to suspend, like any other motion, is carried by a vote of the majority. But, in most deliberative assemblies, there is an established rule on the subject, whereby a motion to suspend, in order to be successful, must have a fixed number of votes; as two-thirds, or three-fourths, for example.

MOTION TO RECONSIDER.

168. *What is a motion to reconsider?*

In the British Parliament, when once a question has been decided, whether negatively, or affirmatively, that decision stands as the sense, will, or judgment of the House, and is held to be irreversible.

But, as the members of an assembly are individually liable to mistakes, so, in their collective capacity, they sometimes find themselves in error. The result is, that in Parliament, where a vote once given is accounted unchangeable, great inconvenience ensues, when it is found, as must occasionally happen, that such vote grew out of error, or misconception.*

The embarrassments resulting from a rigid adherence to this rule have been avoided, in this country, by the introduction of what is called THE MOTION TO RECONSIDER; whereby a decision found to be erroneous, may be reviewed and revised.

* Various are the shifts and expedients adopted in Parliament to escape the consequences of the rule under notice; such as acts explaining, enforcing, correcting, &c., &c.

169. *Under what restrictions, if any, must the motion to reconsider be made?*

The time within which, and the parties by whom, a motion to reconsider shall be made, are, in many cases, fixed by a special rule. Thus, in Congress, a motion to reconsider must be made, either on the same day, or on the day after the passage of the resolution to which it relates. Where there is no special rule on the subject, the motion to reconsider is under no limitation as to time.

In respect to the parties by whom a motion to reconsider shall be made, it is a general rule, that the proposition must emanate from some member who voted with the majority.

170. *In what condition does a motion to reconsider, if decided in the affirmative, place the subject, to which it refers?*

Should a motion to reconsider prevail, the position of the subject, to which it refers, is exactly what it was before the decision which made the reconsideration necessary. It may, therefore, be resumed at that point, and disposed of according to the pleasure of the assembly.

171. *Is the motion to reconsider a privileged one?*

A motion to reconsider in Congress, takes precedence of all other motions, except the motion to adjourn; and, wherever the time within which a motion to reconsider is fixed by special rule, it ought thus to have the precedence.

SECTION VI.

ORDER OF BUSINESS.

172. *When a variety of subjects offer themselves for the consideration of a deliberative body, what particular order, if any, is observed in taking them up?*

In almost all permanently organized bodies, there is a particular order of business established by a special rule, or by-law. But, where no such rule exists, the President, unless the matter is, for the time, otherwise ordered by a vote of the assembly, introduces business according to his pleasure, or sense of propriety in the case.

173. *What advantage, if any, results from a standing rule fixing the order of business?*

A standing rule, or order of business affords several important advantages. It saves time; it secures to each topic its proper place; and, therefore, prevents disputes about precedency, and so facilitates the transaction of business.

174. *Must the standing-rule, or order of business, where there is one, always be adhered to?*

A rule fixing the order of business, like any other rule, may, upon proper occasion, of course, be suspended.

175. *In cases where the minutes of a previous meeting are read, is it necessary to approve them by a formal motion?*

It is quite customary, after the reading of the minutes, for a formal motion of approval to be made and submitted; but such formal action does not appear to be necessary.

For, as they must, if correct, be approved, no motion is needed, unless some error is detected in them. Ordinarily, therefore, where no mistake is discovered, it is quite sufficient for the President to say in substance:—" *What is the pleasure of the meeting in regard to the minutes which have just been read? If there be no objection, they will be considered as approved.*" In the event of there being no objection, he simply adds: " *The minutes, then, stand approved.*"

176. *Suppose an error is detected, what then is done?*

In case of the existence of an error in the minutes, a motion is made to correct, and the correction being made, the President, in submitting the question, says: " *Shall the minutes, as corrected, be approved?*" If decided affirmatively, he simply announces the result, and thus the matter ends.*

177. *What is the next step after the approval of the minutes?*

Immediately after the approval of the minutes, the President announces the first business, in order, accord-

* It should be kept in mind, that no motion to amend the minutes, by striking out words or sentences, is at all admissible, unless they contain some *error of fact.*

ing to the special rule, if there be one, or if not, whatever he deems appropriate first to introduce.

178. *Suppose the first business in order to be the presentation of petitions, memorials, or other communications, in what way are they to be introduced?*

Any member charged with the presentation of a petition, or other communication, should, when the proper time arrives, rise in his place, with the paper in his hand, and announce that he has been commissioned to present such a paper. He then briefly describes the character of the document, and unless anticipated in so doing by another member, moves that it be received.

179. *Is the member who presents such petition, or other communication, responsible, in any wise, for the character of its contents?*

The member that presents a petition or any other communication, should be prepared beforehand to give, if required, a summary of its contents, and to vouch for the decency and respectfulness of its language and sentiments.

180. *Is it in order for parties who are not members of the body, to appear therein, and introduce communications?*

A petition or other communication should always be presented by a member, specially entrusted with that service by the parties from whom it emanates, or by others immediately interested in its contents. But letters and other ordinary communications are usually handed to the President, and by him or by the secretary read without further formality.

181. *If received, what further action is taken upon it?*

If the document be received, it is then handed to the secretary to be read. This being done, the President asks what order shall be taken upon it: whereupon, a motion for that purpose being made, it is either acted upon immediately by the assembly, or set down for a particular time, or referred to a committee, or else postponed indefinitely.

182. *Supposing the next thing in order to be reports from committees, in what way are they to be introduced?*

The time being come for reports from committees, the President, commencing with the first on his list, asks aloud: "*Is the committee on* (naming the subject) *ready to report?*"

The chairman of that committee, if present, or in the event of his being absent, some other member of it, then rises, and, if prepared to report, says: "*The committee, Mr. President, to whom was referred the subject* (naming it) *have had the matter under consideration, and have instructed me to deliver a report, which is ready to be presented whenever the assembly is pleased to receive it.*"*

183. *Is a motion to receive such report necessary?*

No motion to receive the report is necessary, or is generally made, unless some objection to receiving it is raised, or it is deemed expedient to fix some other

* If not prepared to report, he may simply announce, that the committee is not prepared to report at this time, or he may report progress, or make any statement, or explanation respecting the matter which may appear proper or expedient.

time for receiving it. In either case, a motion must be made, and submitted, in the usual way, either by the chairman of the committee himself, or by some other member of the body.

184. *If it be decided to receive the report, what is the next step in the process?*

The report is then, by direction of the President, read,* either by the chairman of the committee in his place, or by the secretary. It is then, together with all other papers connected with it, put in charge of the secretary.

This being done, the President asks: "*What order shall be taken on the report which has just been read?*"

185. *In what way is it proper to respond to this question, or what action does it call forth?*

As an assembly can dispose of a report of a committee just as they can of any other matter proposed for their consideration, the question, "*What order shall be taken on the report?*" elicits, of course, from members motions, either to accept, or adopt, to amend,† to recommit, or to make any other regular disposition of it whatever.

* Where reports are ordered to be printed before being acted upon, as in legislative assemblies, the reading is rendered unnecessary.

† It is, however, a disputed point, whether the report of a committee can be *amended* by the assembly. The best usage seems to be against it. Still, according to high authority, a report may be amended just as well as a resolution. Perhaps, the more courteous way is to re-commit with instructions.

186. *What is the effect of a motion to accept, or adopt, if carried in the affirmative?*

A paper accepted, or adopted by a formal vote of a deliberative assembly, thereby becomes the statement, or sentiment of the assembly itself; for the acts and judgments of the committee, when once adopted in due form, are, by that circumstance, made the acts and judgments of the body, under whose orders they undertook the consideration of the subject.

187. *Would it be out of order to move the acceptance of a report, and the adoption of the resolutions thereto appended, separately.*

It is not only not out of order, but, in fact, the better way, first, to accept the report by a regular motion to that effect, and then adopt the resolutions, if satisfactory, by a separate vote; for, in the resolutions, or recommendations of a committee, indeed, we have a direct expression of the *conclusions* to which they have been led, and therefore a distinct motion to adopt these, as the conclusions of the body at large seems highly proper, if not essential.

188. *What difference of import is there, in this connection, between the terms "accept" and "adopt?"*

Accept and *adopt*, when applied generally to a report, or other document submitted to a deliberative body, are usually understood to denote the same thing; but a more discriminating usage confines the term "*adopt*" to that act by which the assembly directly and distinctly take, and treat as their own the resolutions, or recommendations of a report, or other like document; while the term "*accept*" is employed in relation to papers containing statements of fact, arguments, or reasonings, out of which conclusions are to be educed.

189. *When the report of a committee consists of a paper referred to them for alteration, or amendment, what is the order of proceeding?*

When the report of a committee embraces merely a paper with amendments, the chairman of the committee reads the amendments with the coherence or proper connections, explains the reasons of the alterations, if necessary, and so exhibits, in order throughout, all the changes proposed. The report is then, of course, put in charge of the clerk, or secretary.

When taken up for consideration by the assembly, the amendments only are read by the clerk, or secretary. The President then reads each in course, and submits them successively to a vote of the assembly.

190. *Is it not allowable, during this process, for members to offer other amendments?*

While the assembly is engaged in disposing of amendments proposed by the committee, it is not in order to receive any other amendment, except, of course, an amendment to an amendment, which must then be made, or not made at all.

191. *What opportunity, if any, is allowed for amendments by the assembly?*

The amendments suggested by the committee being decided upon, the President before putting the question on the whole paper, as amended, or not, as the case may stand, waits a moment to hear, if any, other amendments from the assembly, which are then in order.

192. *May a subject on which a report has once been made and presented, be re-committed?*

A subject may be re-committed as often as the assembly please, either to the same, or to a different committee.

193. *When, if ever, is the proper time to hear a report from the minority of a committee?*

The motion to hear the report of the minority should follow immediately the reading of that from the majority. Thereafter, both reports being the property of the house, they may be disposed of according to the pleasure of the assembly.*

194. *If, for any cause, a committee find it inexpedient,*

* On the mode of proceeding respecting a minority report, Mathias (page 38) has the following:—

"Should a committee not be unanimous in opinion, and those in the minority be desirous of placing their views before the meeting, the matter should be introduced immediately after the majority report has been read. A member will then move that 'the report and resolution thereto attached be postponed for the present, for the purpose of enabling the minority to present their report.' If this motion prevails, as is almost always the case, the minority report will be immediately presented, received and read. It is then in order, on motion, to take up for consideration the resolution attached to either of the reports.

"If the minority are not prepared to report, a motion may be made to postpone the majority report until the next meeting, in order to enable the minority to get their report ready."—See answer to question 63, p. 66.

or impracticable, to render a report, what course is taken in relation to such a committee?

When, for any cause, a committee deem it inexpedient to make a report, the chairman, or some other member of that committee should, when the report is called for, rise in his place, and, after making a statement of the case, move that the committee be discharged from the further consideration of the subject.

195. *Supposing a paper consisting of several distinct propositions, or of a series of resolutions, to be laid before an assembly, what order is observed in taking them up?*

In considering a document embracing several propositions, or resolutions, the entire paper should first be read by the secretary. This enables the members to get a general and connected view of the whole matter.

Then, in order the more closely to consider, and, if necessary, to amend each part in detail, the natural order is to begin at the beginning, and go regularly through by paragraphs or resolutions: the President reading each in its turn, and pausing at the end of each to receive and put, if need be, any amendments offered.*

When all this is done, the President submits the whole paper, amended, or unamended, as the case may be, to a vote of the assembly on its final adoption.

* This order is so rigidly adhered to in Parliament that, when the latter part of a paper has been amended, it is not allowable to go back and make alterations in the previous sections, or paragraphs. In the Senate of the United States, however, it is not forbidden to recur to a former part of a paper, under deliberation, for the purpose of amending it.

196. *In the case of a series of resolutions, is it not usual to consider and adopt them separately?*

It is quite common, indeed it is the general custom, in case of a series of resolutions being laid before a deliberative body, to put the question on each resolution separately: the preamble, if any, being reserved, and acted upon last of all.

197. *Why should the preamble be reserved to the last?*

The preamble should be reserved till the resolutions have been disposed of, because in the event of their being amended, it might require alteration to render it appropriate, or should the resolutions be negatived, it would, of course, fall to the ground altogether.

198. *Can more than one subject be under consideration at the same time?*

There can be but one main, or principal subject under consideration in a deliberative assembly at once, but there may be pending at the same time, a number of incidental, or subsidiary questions, all which have been explained already in the answers to questions under the head of Privileged Questions.

199. *When the business of a meeting seems to be finished, what course is taken by the President?*

Whenever a pause or cessation occurs in the proceedings, the President simply says: "*There is no business before the meeting.*" This either brings up new business, or a motion to adjourn.

SECTION VII.

ORDER OF DEBATE.

200. *When is it in order to rise and speak on a motion, or proposition?*

As a motion, or proposition is not fairly before a deliberative assembly, until moved, seconded, and stated from the chair, it is never in order to rise and speak on it, until it has thus formally been introduced.

201. *May the President engage in the debate?*

It being plainly incompatible with a due discharge of his appropriate duties for the President, as a general thing, to take part in the debates, he is not allowed to do so, except in cases growing out of, or naturally belonging to his official position. Thus, he may, and ought, when desirable, to explain points of order; he may give information of facts bearing upon the business under deliberation; and, in the event of an appeal from his decision on questions of order, he is free to engage in any debate thereupon.

When, however, the presiding officer does rise to speak, he is entitled to be heard even before a member who may be already on the floor. In such case, the member standing should take his seat, till the President has finished.

202. *Can a member once fairly in possession of the floor, be refused a hearing?*

He that fairly gets the floor, is fully entitled to be heard. He cannot be interrupted by a call for adjournment, or for the orders of the day, or for the question; for this is not making a regular motion. "Such calls are themselves," says Jefferson, "breaches of order."

203. *In case of a dispute, or of conflicting claims to the floor, who is to decide?*

If several members rise and address the chair at once, or nearly at once, the President is to grant the precedence to him whose voice is first heard. But it is competent for any member to question this decision, and to ask a vote of the assembly thereupon. In case of a vote, the question is first taken on the claim of the member, in whose favor the President has decided.

204. *Is it ever in order to interrupt a member when speaking on a subject before the house?*

It is never in order, as a general rule, to interrupt a member while addressing the house, except by a call to order;* that is, he cannot rightfully be interrupted in his speech by a member rising and proposing to

* It is, in some assemblies, allowable for a member to interrupt a speaker in order to make an explanation.

adjourn, or making any other like privileged motion.*

Yet this rule is not to be so construed or interpreted as to preclude all possible cases or contingences, for such a construction of it would sometimes work greater mischief than that which it is intended to prevent. Thus, cases may arise, in which it may be of the highest moment to interrupt a speaker, in order to announce facts or information of immediate and pressing interest or necessity.

The whole aim of the rule is to secure a member who has the floor, and is speaking, from all wanton or abusive interruption, as long as he himself observes the rules of order and the decencies of debate.

205. *Does a call to order prevent a speaker from finishing his speech?*

When the question raised by a call to order has been decided, the speaker is still in possession of his right to proceed; nor can he be arrested, as before said, even by a motion to adjourn. His right is to a full hearing.

There are some deliberative bodies, in which a rule is laid down, fixing the limits in respect to time, within which every speaker is to be confined. But, even where no such rule exists, a tedious or offensive speaker, though his right to proceed is not questioned, is generally made, by certain indications of impatience in the audience, to see the propriety of closing his speech.

* Sometimes, in order to hasten the decision of a question some member will call out—*Question! Question!* even while a speaker is on the floor. This is usually regarded as the greatest rudeness; though often resorted to in order to get rid of a tiresome speaker.

206. *Is a speaker who, for some special purpose, voluntarily yields the floor in favor af another, entitled as soon as the object of the interruption is gained, to go on with his speech?*

As a matter of *favor*, or *concession*, but not as a matter of *right*, a speaker who temporarily yields the floor in favor of another, is generally permitted, immediately after the interruption, to resume his remarks. If the privilege be denied, he cannot claim it as a right.

207. *Does a person speaking in a deliberative assembly, address himself formally to the assembly, or to the presiding officer?*

Whenever a member of a deliberative assembly proposes to speak upon a matter in debate, he is expected to rise in his place, with head uncovered, and address himself, *in form*, directly to the presiding officer: saying, "*Mr. President, Mr. Chairman,*" or whatever else may be his title in the body. Thereupon the President addresses the speaker by name, and so introduces and commends him to the attention of the meeting.

208. *When a member is speaking, is it in order to designate other members to whom he wishes to refer, by their names?*

It is not in order, neither is it considered in good taste, in debate, for a speaker to designate other members by their names: the modes of expression for this purpose being,—"*The gentleman who has just taken his seat,*" or, "*The member on the other side of the house,*" or, "*The last speaker but one,*" or some other like indication.

209. *What restriction, if any, is a speaker under in regard to the mode of discussing a subject?*

Every speaker is bound to confine himself to the question. This is the common and necessary rule. But it must be liberally interpreted, and never, under color of cutting off digressions, be made to hinder a full and free expression of sentiment.

210. *Under what restrictions, if any, is a speaker, in relation to his mode of treating other members engaged in the debate?*

Every speaker is bound to avoid personalities; that is, he is not to use harsh, reviling, or unmannerly words of any kind in relation to others engaged in the debate; but to exercise, in all respects, a courteous and gentlemanly deportment: principles and measures, not the character and motives of those who advocate them, being the proper subject of animadversion and reprobation.

211. *Under what restriction, if any, is a speaker in respect to his mode of treating the resolves, or other proceedings of the assembly?*

Every speaker is bound to refrain from the use of reproachful or indecent language in regard to the previous acts, or decisions of the assembly, or any of its committees. He may, however, offer and support a motion to rescind any act or resolution of the body, and in so doing, indulge in the language of invective or reprobation, so long as he violates not the rules of debate.

212. *Is it in order for a member to be present, when the assembly are deliberating upon matters, in which he is personally concerned?*

It is neither in order, nor in decency for a member to be present in the assembly, when he is personally interested in the matter under debate.

213. *What, if anything, is done, when a member in addressing the assembly, makes use of language that is insulting to another member, or to the body at large?*

When a member in speaking, indulges in language abusive or insulting to other members, or to the body generally, he is usually interrupted in his speech by members calling him to order. In that case, the party aggrieved, or objecting to the language, is requested by the President, or proceeds of his own accord, either to repeat, or reduce to writing the exact words complained of, so that they may be recorded by the clerk, or secretary.

214. *Must the words be so recorded?*

The words, upon being repeated, may be, or appear to be, less offensive, or insulting than had been supposed. In that event, the President may hesitate, and unless forced by calls to that effect from the assembly, or by a resolution duly passed, he may, in his discretion, allow the affair to pass over by not directing the clerk to take the words down. If that, however, be the clear wish of the assembly, however expressed, the words *must* be recorded, and the matter in due form settled.

215. *Supposing the objectionable words to be taken down by order of the President, or that of the assembly, what follows?*

The words being recorded by the clerk, or secretary, are to be read to the member who is charged with using them; and, if he denies them to be the words which he used, the judgment, or testimony of the assembly is taken by a vote on the question whether the words recorded by the clerk, and imputed to him, be really his, or not. Before taking the question, however, it is competent for the assembly so to amend, or alter the words taken down, as to bring them, if possible, nearer to what, in their judgment, the offending member actually did say.

216. *What if the member does not deny the words?*

If the words imputed be not denied, or if the assembly decides them to be truly reported, the member is at liberty either to justify them, or to show that, as he used them, they are not liable to the charge of being disorderly, or finally, to make such apology as is due under the circumstances. If the justification, or explanation, be deemed satisfactory, or the apology, if he make one, acceptable, there the matter terminates; and he is permitted to resume, and go on with his speech.

217. *How is it ascertained whether, or not the assembly is satisfied with the justification, or explanation, or apology, whichever it may be?*

Whether, in such case, the assembly is satisfied, or

not, is known by their silent acquiescence: the presumption being, that where none object, all agree.

But should any two members insist, that the sense of the body should be taken on the character of the words, or on the guilt or innocence of the person using them, the member must withdraw before that question is stated. After his withdrawal, the question is to be taken, and the penalty, if any, fixed by a vote of the assembly.

218. *Must the complaint against a member for using offensive language, be entered immediately?*

A complaint against a member for using disorderly, or offensive words, must be entered, if at all, at the time the offence is given.* This is a most necessary rule, for if the words be not written down immediately, mistakes will occur, and no security will be afforded to any one against mistaken or malicious charges of disorder.

If, therefore, the speech of another member, or any other business, be allowed to intervene between the time of using the words alleged to be disorderly, and that of making the complaint, such complaint is not to be entertained.

219. *Suppose, at any time, the presiding officer finds it impossible, by calls to order, or appeals to the meeting, to restrain a member, disposed to be disorderly, what is his last resort?*

In case of persistent disorder, on the part of a member, it is the duty of the presiding officer to designate by name the person so behaving and so bring the offender before the assembly.

* Compare however Jefferson and Cushing on this point.

220. *What steps, in such case, may the assembly take?*

The assembly may, and ought to require the member, thus offending, to withdraw: allowing him, however, an opportunity, if he wishes it, to explain, or exculpate himself. Then, after a statement of the nature of the offense from the President, the assembly should decide upon the punishment, if any, due to the transgression.

221. *Suppose the assembly, generally, persist in disorder, what is the President to do?*

If, after proper efforts to preserve order, there is a general and persistent disregard to his appeals and to the character and claims of his office, his obligation further to attempt the control of the meeting, of course, ceases, and he may, therefore, justly abandon the assembly to its own guidance and discretion.

222. *What rule, if any, might prevent the occurrence of a state of things like that supposed in the answer to last question?*

If each individual, whether officer or private member, would but honestly labor to aid the main object of the meeting, which is, or ought to be, the elicitation of truth and the free expression of the ascertained will of the body, such a state of things as that supposed, in the case above, would certainly never occur. The rules of order which have been stated and explained, in the preceding pages, will be found sufficient, if duly observed, to secure the decent and orderly transaction of business in almost any deliberative assembly, provided only the spirit of truth, justice and courtesy prevail among its members.

SECTION VIII.

DEBATING SOCIETIES.

DEBATING Societies, wisely conducted, cannot be too highly commended. They are, indeed, excellent schools; but, like all other schools, good or bad, according to the skill and intelligence with which they are managed. To make them at all subservient to the proper design of their institution, the exercises in them should ever be regarded as important business transactions. They will, indeed, always yield entertainment; but any view of their character, that makes amusement their principal design, cannot fail materially to diminish their utility.

In adopting and signing a written Constitution, each member thereby pledges himself to meet its requirements. It is a *contract*, promising rewards, but imposing obligations. It should, therefore, be faithfully observed; for one, among many things, that may be acquired, or strengthened, in a society of this kind, is the habit of being punctual in the performance of duties. He that habitually violates engagements, voluntarily assumed, however unimportant they may seem, is in danger of falling into precisely the same practice respecting matters of higher moment.

In respect to the discussion and management of questions in general, we have elsewhere* spoken; but there is a class of questions frequently coming up, that seem specially proper to be noticed in this place. I mean questions relating to the provisions, limitations and restrictions, made and imposed in the Constitution and By-Laws† of the Society.

Discussions of this kind, though often avoided, as irksome and profitless, are, when rightly managed, not only interesting, but often highly beneficial. They serve to induce thought in relation to the nature of those fundamental laws and powers in a community, under which, and in conformity with which, all other laws and powers whatever must be made and exercised: dispelling the vagueness that, in youthful minds, almost always attaches to the idea of a Constitution, and habituating them to consider the various distinctions and relations indicated, when we speak of Constitutional, Legislative, Judicial, and Executive powers. It must not, therefore, be thought a waste of time properly to discuss, interpret, and rigidly apply the provisions and requisitions of the Constitution and the

* See page 132.

† The relation of By-Laws to the Constitution is well indicated in the derivation of the term. The term *by-law* or *bye-law* is made up of the word *law*, and the Danish *by* or *bye*, which means a *town*: the combination meaning, literally, *a town-law*. Hence, it signifies generally, a special, or particular law, made by a corporation, or other association to regulate such of their affairs as are not provided for by the general, or constitutional law of the land. By-laws, therefore, confer no new powers, but rather regulate the exercise of those already in existence. For the form of a Constitution and By-Laws for a Debating Society, see Section XIV.

By-Laws; for out of this practice may come habits of mind of the highest service in subsequent life.

Another hint, proper here to be given, is, that, as the object of the Society is the moral and intellectual improvement of its members, no one should be impatient of criticism. Candid criticism cannot be too highly appreciated; that criticism, I mean, that aims to discriminate between the right and the wrong, the good and the bad, the beauties and the deformities of a literary performance. Such criticism, and none other, should ever be indulged, should be sought, not shunned; for by that are we enabled to see and to hear ourselves somewhat, as others see and hear us, and so to follow more closely the path that leads to improvement.

Were it necessary to produce examples illustrative of the beneficial influence of debating societies, it would be no difficult task to cite many great names,—names of men who, in early life, eagerly availed themselves of the advantages of organizations of this nature. The able and dignified Lord Mansfield, for instance, found in a debating society, wherein many legal questions were discussed, the motive to those extensive and accurate preparations which, in subsequent years, became so highly valuable in his illustrious career.

Edmund Burke, perhaps, the greatest deliberative orator that ever appeared on the floor of the British House of Commons, is known to have sought discipline in the matter of public speaking, in the exercises of a debating society.

Charles Fox, who, according to Burke, rose "by slow degrees to be the most brilliant and accomplished debater the world ever saw," was so sensible of the advantage of regular and frequent practice, that he actually turned the House of Commons into a sort of Debating Club for his own personal benefit; that is, he often entered earnestly, as he himself confesses, into the discussion of questions which involved for him no other or higher interest than that of affording discipline in debate.

Curran, the most unpromising of all aspirants after fame in oratory, (Demosthenes not excepted,) derived from debating societies the stimulus and the discipline by which, in great measure, he ultimately took rank among the first of orators. Awkward and ungainly in gesture, hasty and inarticulate in utterance, he labored long and labored hard, with no other result, apparently, than that of earning the titles, "*Stuttering Jack*" and "*Orator Mum.*" But his failures were really only so many pledges of success; for the process of improvement, silent, but sure, was all the while going steadily on.

Henry Clay, a name that at once awakens the recollection of everything that is, either forceful, or fascinating in deliberative eloquence, gained, as is well known, no small advantage from his active participation in the exercises of a debating society.

But further specification is needless. Reason and experience alike attest the value of well-regulated bodies of this description; and he is not wise, who disregards testimony so important and so conclusive.

SECTION IX.

MANAGEMENT OF A QUESTION.

IN all cases, where time is allowed for the study of a question previously to its actual discussion, it is, of course, the dictate of wisdom to consider carefully beforehand how it should be managed.

Discussion * implies thorough investigation. It cannot be effected without labor; but, when properly done, it amply repays the laborer, by establishing in him those habits of inquiry and discrimination, which are constantly demanded in the questions of real life. In order to aid the young debater in the work of preparation, we offer the following general directions.†

Of all the sources of idle discussion, imprecision in

* The word *discussion*, is from the Latin *discutio*, which is itself made up of DIS, *apart*, and QUATIO, *to shake*: signifying, of course, *the shaking apart*, that is, the thorough sifting, or examination of a subject.

† These directions, though they embrace some things that have regard to the manner and bearing of a debater towards his opponent, do not, and are not intended to cover the ground occupied by what is usually treated of under the head of the "Order of Debate." For remarks, therefore, on the use of personalities and other indecorous conduct in debate, see page 123 and following.

the use of language is, perhaps, the most prolific. Hence, the first step towards the right management of a question, is to clear it of all verbal obscurity, that is, put it in language the plainest and most precise practicable.

But a question may be stated in a manner sufficiently intelligible, and, after all, be misunderstood, or not understood at all, for want of reasonable regard to the meaning, or application of particular terms. A second direction, therefore, not less important than the first, is to ascertain by study the exact signification of every leading term in the question. Dr. Watts, in speaking on this subject, says:—"This is so necessary a thing, that, without it, men will be exposed to such sort of ridiculous contests, as was found one day between two unlearned combatants, Sartor and Sutor, who assaulted and defended the doctrine of *Transubstantiation* with much zeal and violence. But Latino happening to come into their company, and inquiring the subject of their dispute, asked each of them what he meant by that long, hard word *Transubstantiation*. Sutor readily informed him, that he understood it bowing at the name of Jesus. But Sartor assured him, that he meant nothing but bowing at the high altar. 'No wonder,' then said Latino, 'that you cannot agree, when you neither understand one another, nor the word about which you contend.'"

The world has always been full of Sartors and Sutors, that is, people fond of debate, but often "understanding neither what they say, nor whereof they affirm."* He that will not study to avoid their error, can never reasonably hope to be a good debater.

* 1 Timothy, ch. i., v. 9.

Another direction, which has often been given, but which cannot be too earnestly inculcated, is to ascertain precisely the aim of the question, and keep it always steadily in view. Digression is the *ignis fatuus* of discussion. It misleads by the appearance of utility: luring the mind into devious paths, and dissipating its powers in idle pursuit. We should guard against it in ourselves, because it is hostile to the best exercise of the reasoning faculty. We should guard against it in others, because it wastes time, fatigues an audience, and—sometimes by chance, sometimes by design—defeats the only proper end of discussion—the elicitation of truth.

The language of the question being clear, and clearly understood, and the precise point of investigation fairly before the mind, the next thing is to consider carefully what may be said on both sides. Assume, for the time being, the position of an opponent; endeavor to produce and appreciate at its full value, every argument likely to be employed against you, and so compare in detail the strength and resources of your own side with those of your adversary.

This will prevent you from being suddenly surprised by the presence and power of unexpected arguments, and give you all the advantage of seeming to know beforehand what is coming out on the opposite side. It will inspire respect in your adversaries, and impart caution to their modes of attacking your positions, and so leave on the minds of the audience the silent, but strong impression of probability, as belonging to what you affirm.

If it be necessary to elucidate, or confirm your views

by reference to history, geography, statistics, or anything else derivable from books, be accurate, to the last degree, in whatever you quote or state, as matter of fact. This is a most important precept. Minute accuracy begets confidence. It lends to the speaker the charm of reliability. Many a man who has no other merit scarcely, is always heard with decided interest, because he is known to be scrupulously exact in his statements.

Having duly considered the question, and collected all the materials which you propose to employ in the debate, the next thing is to *arrange* them to the best advantage. "Every mind," says an able writer, "instinctively requires order," and to this we add, that no man can ever succeed, as an orator, who disregards this instinct of our nature. *What* particular order, however, shall, in any given case, be adopted, must, as a matter of course, be left to your own discretion. Whatever it is, let it be clear; and, when once indicated, adhere to it throughout. This will enable your hearers to follow you with ease, to remember your positions, and measure accurately the force of your arguments.

Another direction, that will be found extremely useful, if duly regarded, is, always to treat the arguments of your opponents with fairness and courtesy. Nothing is ever gained by affecting to treat what is said by those opposed to you, with disdain, or by perverting their views, or by seeking to undervalue their force.

The better way always is to allow what is due to the opposite side, and show, if possible, its weakness by clear, forcible, and convincing argumentation. There is force in fairness; for it implies a love of truth.

There is power in politeness; for it moves the heart, and begets the impression of a generous adversary.

The last precept which we shall here endeavor to inculcate, is always to seem sincere in the search after truth. In order, however, to *seem* sincere, you must really *be* so; for sincerity is a coin hard to be counterfeited. Be the copy ever so skillfully executed, it will always fall far short of the original, and always, consequently, be more or less liable to detection.

Every hollow profession, when once fairly detected, is justly treated as an act of imposition. Even the suspicion of insincerity is prejudicial, in the highest degree, if not absolutely fatal, to the influence of a public speaker. In debate, therefore, as in all the other transactions of life, the maxim is fully verified,—"Honesty is the best policy."

But a most serious hinderance to the virtue which we are here commending, is found in obstinacy,—a quality usually in close alliance with ignorance and vanity. Goldsmith's country schoolmaster is a character which, in the feature now under notice, is often realized in all human circles and professions:—

> "In arguing, too, the parson owned his skill,
> For, e'en though vanquished, he could argue still."

SECTION X.

DEBATES IN FULL.

UNDER this head we here insert a couple of debates, for the purpose of affording a sort of practical illustration of the mode of conducting a public discussion. They are, however, in no sense set up as *models*, in respect to style, expression, or logic. Theirs is an humbler, though a useful aim. They are designed simply to impart, or indicate something of the form and spirit of those real transactions which almost daily occur in deliberative assemblies. They are merely *suggestive.*

These debates may be used as exercises in declamation, each speaker being represented by a different person. In such case, moreover, the speakers might be encouraged to add to, or amplify the arguments and illustrations in their several parts, and so give a sort of original interest to the exercise. Especial care should be taken to preserve the formalities and the decorum proper to the occasion; for these are things that become familiar only by practice.

DEBATE.

WHICH IS THE MORE PERNICIOUS CHARACTER, THE SLANDERER OR THE FLATTERER?

FIRST SPEAKER.

Mr. President,—It will not, I hope, be thought captious in me, if I venture to intimate my doubts about the wisdom of *proposing* such a question, as that which is to form the topic of this discussion. If, in so doing, I should be considered as intentionally impugning the judgment, or wounding the feelings of those whose province it is to furnish us with subjects of debate, I should be sadly misinterpreted. I beg leave, therefore, in the outset, to disclaim any and every purpose of disparagement, that might be inferred from the position which I take on the present occasion.

Evil speaking, sir, which is the Bible expression for slander, is a crime of the darkest character; so much more heinous than flattery, that it seems almost like sharing in the guilt of slander to assume, as this question does, that the two things differ from each other so slightly, as to make it difficult to determine their comparative iniquity and enormity.

Slander, Mr. President, is among the most cruel, as it certainly is among the most criminal things in the world. It justly ranks, in the common estimation, with theft and with murder; and often, therefore, in metaphor, does it bear these odious names. Nothing, accordingly, is more common, even in prose, to say nothing of poetry, than such expressions as, "to rob one of his good name," "to stab one's reputation:" *stealing*, *stabbing* and *slandering* being, it would seem, closely allied in guilt, and naturally associated in the mind.

Though these, sir, are my views of slander, I would not, on that account, have you imagine, that I stand here as the apologist of flattery. On the contrary, I am prepared, on every proper occasion, to condemn this latter vice in terms quite as severe as the most rigid moralist could either wish, or require.

Still, sir, that would not prove the justice of the comparison here instituted. Flattery is bad; slander is bad; but are they equally bad, or so nearly alike in power for mischief, as to warrant serious doubts about their comparative malignity? Certainly not.

In the flatterer, generally, you find no evil intent. His conduct exhibits weakness, rather than wickedness; weakness deplorable, indeed, but not altogether unamiable. In the slanderer, on the contrary, you may always detect the presence of malignant principle,—the pointed, premeditated purpose to work the ruin of character. Like the race whose wickedness brought destruction by the flood, "every imagination of the thoughts of his heart is only evil continually."*

Even in their mildest developments, these two characters differ immeasurably. There is a flattery, moving gently, and only by implication; there is a slander, moving secretly, and only by insinuation. The former is delicate, not venturing to appear in words. The latter is cunning, not daring to deal in direct accusa-

* Genesis, ch. vi., v. 5.

tion. The one is cheerful, and hopes to win by the appearance of admiration. The other is grave, and calculates to succeed by an air of mystery. In the one, you see the semblance of deference and candor; in the other, you observe the look of shrewdness and watchful suspicion. The one bows, it may be, with simulated reverence; the other shrugs the shoulder, and labors to *act* out the villany which he has not the courage to *utter*.

But, sir, I feel that, in pursuing this comparison, I am, as it were, doing violence to reason: undertaking to force the application of a standard which is obviously illiberal and unjust. To me, the question seems not only far-fetched, but absurd. It is comparing mountains with mole-hills. It is asking whether the bite of a flea is more fatal than that of a mad dog; whether the mosquito infuses a poison more subtle and deadly than that of the rattlesnake; whether flakes of fleecy snow, gently falling on the traveller's head, are more terribly destructive than the weight and might of the irresistible avalanche.

It may be, sir, that I am mistaken in this view of the case. If so, I hope soon to be enlightened. But, with my present convictions, right or wrong, I can see nothing to dispute about. There is no debatable ground in the question; at least, so it seems to me, and, for that reason, I shall take my seat, and wait, as befits me, the issue of that light, whencesoever it may come, that is destined to confirm, or overthrow the conclusion I have reached.

SECOND SPEAKER.

Mr. President,—The gentleman to whom we have just listened, finds, it seems, no sufficient ground of comparison between slander and flattery. He wonders, why such a question should ever have been introduced, and seems really afraid, lest, by the formal discussion of it, our reputation, if not for sanity, at least for soundness of judgment, may be seriously impaired.

I do not, sir, I must say, share with him in his amiable solicitude, and, therefore, hope sincerely that this debate, which he so much deprecates, may, at least, prove equal to the task of removing all his painful forebodings.

I am far, sir, from thinking with him, that slander and flattery are divided by such immeasurable dissimilarity. With him, flattery wears many objectionable features; but, after all, she is not utterly vile. There is, he appears to think, something of fascination in her air, something of sweetness in her tones and modulations, nay, something even of benevolence in her disposition, which wonderfully atones for all her defects and delinquencies.

In slander, however, he finds nothing but evil, unmixed and unmitigated. It is to him what Polyphemus was to the terrified Trojans,—

"Monstrum horrendum, informe, ingens."*

Now, sir, I am inclined to regard this view of the

* A monster terrible, deformed, and huge.

case, as hasty; founded rather in first impressions and particular prejudices, than in any careful and profound analysis of the things themselves. Flattery seems, so to speak, to have struck his fancy. He, accordingly, views her only in the distance, and, as here, as elsewhere, "distance lends enchantment to the view," he is captivated with the semblance of excellence, or, at least, softened by the smiling, but deceptive aspect of truth and candor, which she wears.

But, sir, be not deceived. Bring this fair creature into nearer view. Take off her smooth disguises, and resolve all her plausibilities into plain matter of fact; then place her side by side with slander, and you will be astonished to find in these two characters, not only similarity, but absolute identity. Both originate in the spirit of deception. Alike in essence and in aim, they go forth, differing only in outward accidents and circumstances, deceiving, and to deceive continually.

It is idle, then, sir, to dwell upon the pleasing aspects of flattery, as constituting higher claims to innocence than those that may be urged in favor of slander. These seductive charms, rightly interpreted, are only so many withering blasts of testimony against her. Is the poison which is sweet less fatal than that which is bitter? Was the bite of the asp, though it worked by slow degrees, and gentle stupefaction, less fatal to Cleopatra, than would have been that of the more malignant adder, which advances by rapid steps and violent convulsions?

But again, sir, I say, be not deceived. If flattery is to be excused, or palliated on the ground of external appearances, I am for extending the same favor to slander. *It*, also, has its fair side, its ingenuous air, its agreeable professions.

The slanderer is no novice in the arts of pretension. He covers his iniquity in the most judicious and skillful manner. If there be merit in a mask, he is fully equal to the flatterer in the ease and dexterity, with which he assumes and wears that article. He has the show of public virtue. He affects to believe what he affirms, and for the sake of others, he seems ready to risk the perils that ever belong to the exposer of vicious persons. His position is that of a friend warning us against danger. He often leads us to regard him as the best friend of virtue, because he appears to be the most fearless denouncer of vice. In short, he plays the hypocrite. But this is exactly what the flatterer is doing all the while; and, in this, if he excels the slanderer, he thereby only proves, that, for all the purposes of mischief, he is more facile and fertile in expedients.

I have thus, sir, I hope, shown you, that slander and flattery, so far from being utterly unlike, are really identical in essence, and alike, also, in some of their more important manifestations. If this be so, then is the question before us not liable to the critical objections, which have been started against it,—then may we proceed, in the discussion, without serious apprehension about the safety of our reputation for judgment and discrimination.

Having disposed of the gentleman's cavils and arguments, as best I could, I beg leave to close my remarks by directing your attention to one peculiar trait of the flatterer, wherein he seems to me to surpass incomparably every degree of enormity, of which the most willful slanderer is capable. It is this: the slanderer attacks, perhaps ruins, your *reputation;* but the flatterer assaults, and is most certain to destroy your *character.* Character, you know, sir, is what we *are;* reputation what we *seem*, or are *said* to be.

The slanderer seeks to injure us in the estimation of others. He often succeeds in his purpose; but, if we are guiltless of his charges, if we are really pure in heart and pure in hand, though our reputation may be injured, our character is still unhurt. We have the *mens conscia recti*, the mind conscious of the right, which enables us to rejoice even in the midst of suffering. Aristides was driven from his native country by a successful assault upon his reputation, and Socrates drank the fatal hemlock, because of similarly foul aspersions; but both being pure in character, and strong in conscious virtue, the one only prayed, that his country might never be in circumstances to need his return, while the other, instead of quailing under the near approach of death, calmly assured his infatuated judges, "*that an honest man needs to fear no evil, either in this, or the future life.*"

But, sir, the flatterer aims at a nearer and a dearer object. He studies out "the soft approaches of the heart," watches its weaker inclinations, and gently insinuates the baneful seeds of vanity. By this subtle process, the understanding is gradually darkened, the judgment is warped, conceit is taken for actual attainment, and all the foundations of solid worth are effectually undermined. Thence comes the custom, and out of that the habit, of seeking in pretension a substitute for possession, accepting the praise, without having the reality of merit, and, in a word, relying for success and for satisfaction on a reputation unsupported by correspondent character,—the shadow, instead of the substance, of virtue.

This, sir, is the legitimate consequence of successful flattery. If slander tarnish our good name, we may hope to brighten it again by dint of good living; but if, by the hand of flattery, however fair, however delicate, the fountains of good living be themselves roiled and poisoned, whence, O whence, shall the deluded soul look for the means of retrievement?

THIRD SPEAKER.

Mr. President,—I listened with pleasure to the member who has just addressed us; but not with the pleasure that results from satisfaction with a sound course of argument. If clearness of diction were always synonymous with soundness of logic, I should doubtless be tempted, by the seemingly transparent view of the case, which he has presented, to yield the position which he claims in this discussion.

He assumes, without a shadow of proof, that all flattery is designed to do mischief. It is by this assumption, in great measure, that he is enabled to complete his view of the absolute identity of slander and flattery. But for this, the parallel would not hold out.

Now, sir, here I must take issue with him. I deny, that flattery uniformly aims at mischief to the party flattered. On the contrary, nothing can be more certain, than that, in most cases, as intimated by the opening speaker, the motive of the flatterer is a kind, a benevolent one. I do not say,—I do not mean to say, that this is the best, or even a good way, of exercising kindly feeling. I merely note the fact.

If this be so, and I see not how it can be reasonably controverted, then, sir, the argument derived from it remains yet unanswered. And that argument seems to me quite irresistible; for the notion of kindly intention is altogether incompatible with the idea of slander. In a thousand ways, may flattery be employed, with comparative innocence, if not with positive advantage; in not one is it possible to conceive of slander without guilt of the deepest dye.

The mother, watching with fond anxiety the first efforts of her child to walk, to sing, to read, to do anything yet unlearned or unattempted, may innocently, we should think, encourage hope and stimulate exertion by the use of flattering words. The teacher whose task is to study all those arts, by which the youthful mind is roused to energy and perseverance in the pursuit of knowledge, can hardly be denied the agency ot flattering expressions of approbation in the prosecution of his arduous duties. Shall the generous youth, ambitious of high civil or military distinction, no longer find encouragement in the song of grateful adulation, or the speech that deals in lofty panegyric? Shall all the agreeable courtesies of society be forever relinquished, because they are denounced as the offspring of flattery?

It is not, then, sir, too much to assume, that flattery is frequently found not a little beneficial in its operation. It may, it is true, be employed for wicked purposes; but that, sir, may be affirmed of almost every thing. We do not surely require to be reminded, that the abuse of a thing is not to be taken as an argument against the legitimate use of it. That which, rightly used, is known to be a wholesome food or an efficacious remedy, is often equally well known to be, in rash or ignorant hands, a most deadly poison.

The gentleman dwells upon the seductive arts of flattery, the engaging manner which she assumes, in order to accomplish her purposes. Well, in that he is certainly right. She is doubtless fair in form, and in possession of many attractive graces. But is not this an odd sort of objection? Without these arts and graces, would she *be* flattery at all? If his objection, therefore, be resolved into its ultimate essence, it will be, that he objects to flattery, because it *is* flattery. So do we all; but what has that to do with the immediate question before us?

But his design evidently is to gain something, in this argument, by lingering upon the false, though fair, features of flattery, as though slander were a creature of honest countenance, and manly bearing, and altogether above petty deceptions. But what, sir, is the reality of the case? Does the gentleman require again to be informed, that slander is quite as plausible as flattery?

When Iago proceeds to awaken the cruel suspicions of Othello, what guise does he assume but that of friendship? The odious mask of friendship, so well preserved in the character of Iago, is scarcely less revolting to our better feelings, than the foul aspersions which he breathes, or insinuates against the guiltless Desdemona. This scene, in the great Dramatist, is realized every day in the actual drama of life. "What God hath joined together, let no man put asunder," is the solemn injunction of Holy Writ; but here is a creature, in form, a man, in fact, a demon, who, regardless alike of the laws of earth, and the prohibitions of Heaven, takes the guise of disinterested friendship, and, under that guise, works, by the excitation of rage and jealousy, the utter dissolution of the marriage bond, and the utter destruction of helpless innocence.

Yet, the gentleman talks about the fair, but deceptive forms of flattery. What form, sir, more fair, or more deceptive, *can* the flatterer assume, than that of the viperous Iago, when he worked upon the suspicions of the jealous Moor?

But, sir, I see the slanderer in other scenes. Here is a youth, high in promise, elate in spirits, breathing all the fullness and freshness of early hope. He is honest, active, intelligent, industrious, competent every way. He has ventured to establish a business of his own. He has labored long and assiduously, for one so young, to deserve the confidence of his fellow-men. This only he needs to secure success in his new undertaking. But he has competitors. These, if only the rivalry were generous, might serve rather to energize than to enfeeble his efforts.

But there is one who is determined to defeat him. All at once, in a quarter vital to his prosperity, some adverse influence begins to operate. What can it be, that thus secretly affects his credit? What oversight in trade, what imprudence in expenditure, what appearance of extravagance, has been discovered, or imagined? Why, why are the former facilities so suddenly, so absolutely, cut off? These questions start up in the doubting, disappointed soul. They harass by day; they make sleepless his night; they wound his pride; they crush ambition; they generate all gloomy imaginings; and when, perchance, the hour of reparation is forever past, all at once he learns, that what eluded his search, though it ruined his business, was nothing more nor less than the poisonous breath of the secret slanderer.

In this latter case, as in the former, sir, the slanderer is supposed to operate successfully, only because of an ingenious mask. He would guard a friend against the snares of an unworthy debtor; he had no secret grudge, or evil motive of any kind; not he. It was pure, disinterested friendship. This was the pretense, the smooth outside, which the treacherous transaction was made to assume.

Now, sir, since this matter of appearances has been so prominently urged, I insist upon your comparing these disguises of slander with those attributed to the flatterer. Are those of the former less ingenious, less imposing, less effective any way, than those of the latter? I leave your own judgment, your own conscience, to answer.

I might, Mr. President, proceed to give other illustrations of this point; but I feel it to be unnecessary. I am satisfied that you will, and must, agree with me in the conclusion, that whatever covering they may put on, whatever air they may assume, whatever language they may adopt, these two odious characters differ from each other most widely, in this, that the slanderer far outstrips the flatterer in the production of deep and lasting detriment.

FOURTH SPEAKER.

Mr. President,—The considerations offered by the last speaker certainly seem somewhat forcible. Their force is, however, I think, mainly apparent. It grows rather out of a certain ingenuity of statement, than out of any real power in the argumentation itself.

Does not all that he has urged, amount just to this? There is *nothing* good in slander; there *is* something good in flattery; *ergo*, slander is worse than flattery.

This short syllogism comprehends the burden of his speech; on this he seems fully to rely, as the lawyers say, for a verdict in his favor. The syllogism, too, looks like a valid one. It has, indeed, somewhat the air of that flattery which he here advocates. Yet, sir, its validity, after all, is merely apparent, as I hope to show you.

In all reasoning, direct or indirect, in order to render a conclusion satisfactory, there must be no uncertainty about the premises. But are the premises, in the present instance, perfectly clear and satisfactory?

It has already been shown by a previous speaker, that slander and flattery both equally and essentially originate in the spirit of deception. To call things by their right names, they are only different phases of lying. Every slander is a lie,—every flattery is a lie. This may seem strange language in this place; it may sound harsh, and even coarse, to ears polite. But, sir, is it not true?

Assuming this to be true,—for I see not how it can be otherwise considered,—how, I ask, can it be shown, that falsehood, when it appears in the shape of slander, has *no* good in it, but the moment it takes the guise of flattery, it has *some* good in it? Will it not be necessary, in order to give validity to the gentleman's argument, to prove, beyond the shadow of a doubt, that good is sometimes found in lying? And, for that purpose, will it not further be necessary to demonstrate, and that in the very face of Holy Scripture, that "a lying tongue" is *not* one of the six things hated of the Lord?* For, surely, sir, God cannot hate good in any form.

The fact is, Mr. President, flattery is falsehood, and slander is falsehood, and there is no good in either. Take, therefore, out of the gentleman's syllogism the words *slander* and *flattery*, and insert in each place the word *lying*, which is the proper equivalent, and its fallacy will immediately appear. It will then stand thus: There is *no* good in *lying;* but there is *some* good in *lying; ergo, lying* is worse than *lying!*

Surely, sir, the gentleman does not hope to convince by reasoning like this. He must, on the contrary, consent to bring the two characters, named in the question, into fair comparison. They are both deceivers, both entitled to high distinction for works of wickedness. Yet they differ widely in their power, and tendency to evil. Let us, therefore, adhere to the real point in dispute. That point is simply—which of these two confessedly pernicious characters, is the *more* pernicious?

Now, I maintain, that the arts, or means employed by the flatterer, enable him to do greater mischief, and

* Proverbs, ch. vi., ver. 16, 17, 18.

that, in general, he does do greater mischief, than the slanderer ever can do by any possibility whatever. The world is full of the memorials of flattery's ruinous agency.

When Milton sang

> "Of man's first disobedience, and the fruit
> Of that forbidden tree, whose mortal taste
> Brought death into the world, and all our woe,"

he sang of the terrible consequences of flattery. Alas! poor Eve, though in thy disobedience we recognize the source of all human calamity, we cannot but sympathize with thee, when wavering under the tempting tongue of the flatterer. Who, who might have withstood that subtle and seductive strain? Even as it appears in the fancy of the poet, there is a charm about it that makes us lend a willing ear, and even forget for a moment, that we are listening to the voice of the Devil:

> "Fairest resemblance of thy Maker fair!
> Thee all things living gaze on, all things thine
> By gift, and thy celestial beauty adore
> With ravishment beheld! there best beheld
> Where universally admired; but here
> In this inclosure wild, these beasts among,
> Beholders rude, and shallow to discern
> Half what in thee is fair, one man except,
> Who sees thee? (and what is one?) who should'st be seen
> A Goddess among Gods, adored and served
> By angels numberless, thy daily train."

"So glozed* the Tempter," adds the inimitable poet.

* *Gloze* is formed from *gloss*, just as *glaze* is formed from *glass*. *Gloss*, in Greek γλῶσσα, *the tongue*, is used to signify a note, com-

"So *glozed* the Tempter!" What word, in all the languages of earth, could so well describe this diabolical transaction? "So glozed the Tempter!" It was by *glozing*, that is, by flattering with the *tongue*, that the foul fiend contrived, in the person of Eve, to achieve the ruin of the race. How many, many thousands of her fair descendants have since been ruined by the same hellish agency, what tribunal, save that of the final judgment, can ever, ever disclose?

The cup of Circe and the song of the Sirens, in the old mythology, both admirably symbolize the combined fairness and foulness of flattery. It is delightful to the taste, but brutalizing to the taster; it is enchantment to the ear, but death to the hearer. Virtue often derives vigor from the assaults of slander, but where is the vigilance which flattery may not surprise, or where is the firmness which flattery may not undermine? How many kings, statesmen, heroes and celebrities of every name, whom neither the might of armies, nor the money of a Crœsus could ever subdue, or purchase, have yielded themselves willing captives to the power of a delusive tongue? How many communities, whom no threat of tyranny, no promise of bounty, could, for one instant, induce to tolerate the exercise of despotic rule, have, by the influence of cajoling demagogues, been subjected to a despotism more odious than that of Dionysius, more infamous than that of the Cæsars?

ment, or explanation; thence, also, a specious, or artful interpretation, and, by easy transition, brightness, or superficial lustre. Gloze, therefore, is literally *to tongue over* anything, that is, to invest it with a smooth and fair outside; to delude by flattery.

Sir, a life of virtue is the death of slander. He that is upright in principle, and circumspect in walk and conversation, is generally beyond the reach of permanent injury from the touch of slander. But what discourages and defeats the purposes of slander, often invites the stealthy approach of flattery.

The slanderer stands at a distance, and endeavors to bring ruin upon us from abroad. The policy of flattery is to make us work out our own destruction. It deals in traps, pitfalls, and snares of every description. It is a sort of moral chloroform, that steals away the senses, and disarms the soul.

"Faithful are the *wounds* of a friend," says Solomon, "but the *kisses* of an enemy are deceitful;" and, sir, compared with flattery, slander *is* a friend,—one that, at least, keeps us on our guard, making us watchful, however undesignedly, against whatever act, or indulgence might justly expose us to the tongue of animadversion.

But, sir, I will not longer trespass upon your patience. The matter in dispute is too clear to need further explanation, and its decision will, I hope, serve to show, that you fully concur with me in the opinion, that whatever be the magnitude of the slanderer's guilt, that of the flatterer is greater still.

FIFTH SPEAKER.

Mr. President,—I am little versed in metaphysical speculations. In truth, I have very little taste in that direction. You will not, therefore, expect me to linger long, either on the lines of essential distinction, if any there be, between slander and flattery, or upon the proofs of their original and generic identity, supposing that view of the case to be the true one.

"Well," exclaims some one, "but what disposition will you make of the argument founded upon the consideration, that they are both essentially *deceivers.* Are they not alike in guilt, as they are alike in nature? Will it not be indispensable to go somewhat into what you call 'metaphysical speculation,' in order to satisfy the demands of the discussion?"

To all this I answer,—suppose I accept, as I really do, the doctrine that the slanderer and the flatterer both spring from the same parents, that is, both have their origin in a lying spirit. What will that prove? It is only by operating upon the principle, that he that offendeth in *one* point, is guilty of the *whole*, a declaration that respects the perfect law of God, and which makes *all* sin equally an infringement of the Divine commandments, that you can derive anything like an argument from the assumed identity of slander and flattery.

Still, let us apply that standard. What is the result? Why, since every sin is, according to the hypothesis, equal to every other sin, it follows, that the inherent guilt of these two things is precisely equal. But granting them to be equal, in this respect, what do you gain by the disclosure? The question is not, which is the more wicked character by nature, but which, by the exercise of that wickedness, produces the greater mischief.

Well, now it does seem to me, that a lie that is merely complimentary, cannot be so deleterious as one that is abusive and malicious. There are many people who, without the least evil intent, nay, with the best intentions possible, are always seeking to say kind things, though they may be somewhat exaggerated. They are, indeed, lavish sometimes in the use of complimentary terms. But we never, on that account, think of dealing harshly with them. We regard the intention, and look with indulgence, if not with approbation, upon the motive that governs their conduct.

But how is it, in the case of him who puts forth the language of calumny? What mitigation comes, or can come, from considering *his* motive? What kindly impulse, what benevolent end, throws, or ever can throw, over his vicious career the mantle of all-bearing, all-believing, all-hoping Charity? We can have no conception of slight slander, or inoffensive defamation. It would be a solecism in terms, to speak of such a thing. Slander is never slight, never inoffensive, because were it so, it would no longer *be* slander. The poison which it discharges, is always of the most fatal character.

How differently do slander and flattery appear in the eyes of the Legislator! We often hear of suits and trials for slander; but who has ever heard of suits and trials for flattery? There is an *argument* in this fact. Were flattery equally deleterious with slander, it certainly would have been ranked among penal offenses in the Statute Book. Instead of that, it takes ground with those numerous vices which, being considered too slight, or too subtle to be reached by the arm of the Legislator, are necessarily handed over to the pen of the Satirist, that is, to the potent voice of public Opinion.

The law, in this particular, no doubt, as in all others, is governed somewhat by the *quo animo*, the secret purpose, the motive. It compares the *hearts* of these two characters, as well as the outward workings and consequences of their action. On this ground, undoubtedly, in great measure, it punishes the one with exemplary damages, while it dismisses the other, not as altogether guiltless, but as properly belonging to a more indulgent tribunal.

This interior view of the slanderer's character, Mr. President, may, perhaps, help more than anything else to bring us to a just decision of the point in dispute.

Take a faint picture of the slanderer's head and heart, —the secret chambers of his soul, when he proceeds to operate in his appropriate sphere. See Memory, Reason, Judgment, Imagination, Hope, Fear, Envy, Malice, Hatred, Pride, Vanity, Selfishness, all the powers and passions assembled in secret conclave against virtue and innocence. See Memory furnishing facts and circumstances; see Reason and Judgment, the distinguishing attributes of our common humanity, forced into the debasing office of constructing false and sophistical arguments; see Imagination busily engaged in moulding the vilest fancies into the forms of reality; see Hope, even Hope, that should ever be the sweet solace of misery and misfortune, smiling complacently and promising success to the foulest conspiracy; see Fear whispering caution, Envy exulting in the prospective calamity of a neighbor, Malice joining hand with Hatred to infuse the bitter poison of antipathy; while Pride, Vanity, and Selfishness, creatures one in spirit, and different only in their modes of manifestation, combine their energies for the encouragement and consummation of the diabolical enterprise.

But, sir, I would not seek further to depict this "Stygian Council,"—this perfect Pandemonium of the soul. But what, what, I ask, must be the measure of that iniquity, that can combine for the execution of its purposes, forces, moral and intellectual, so opposite and incongruous as these?

One more thought, Mr. President, and I will bring my observations to a close. That thought is, that a very reliable argument in favor of the side which I here advocate, might be drawn from the testimony of the wise and good of all ages and countries.

I have not the testimony at hand, of course; and, if I had, it would be altogether too voluminous to offer in detail, as you know. But I venture to affirm, that could this be done, their views would confirm mine, with scarcely a dissentient voice. One example only I can now recall from among the ancients; but that indicates, I doubt not, the spirit that pervades them all. Diogenes, the famous old Cynic, being asked, on a certain occasion, of which beast the bite was the most dangerous, immediately answered, "If you mean *wild* beasts, it is the slanderer's; if *tame*, the flatterer's!"

In this answer of Diogenes, I recognize the fair, unbiassed judgment of mankind. With him, the slanderer instantly takes the features, traits, characteristics, or what not, that belong peculiarly to the wild, ferocious beast of prey, compared with which, the flatterer is a creature tame, gentle, and harmless.

Do not, sir, misunderstand me. I am not advocating the claims of flattery to moral purity; for it has none.

On the contrary, I see clearly and regret deeply its sad delinquency. But, if asked whether it exceeded, in my opinion, the measure of wrong-doing that belongs to slander, I could, with a clear conscience, and with a firm voice, adopt for answer the words of the immortal Shakspeare:

> "No; 'tis slander,
> Whose edge is sharper than the sword, whose tongue
> Outvenoms all the worms of Nile; whose breath
> Rides on the posting winds, and doth belie
> All corners of the world: kings, queens, and states,
> Maids, matrons, nay, the secrets of the grave,
> This viperous slander enters."

SIXTH SPEAKER.

Mr. President,—The labor of our opponents, in this debate, has thus far been directed, it would seem, to the purpose of giving to flattery the aspect of a very venial offense. This has been attempted in two ways; first, by dwelling upon the deformities of slander, and so filling the mind with a sense of its enormity, as effectually to exclude, for the time, the idea of equal wickedness in flattery; secondly, by painting flattery in colors calculated to conceal, rather than display her real character: presenting her in the form of a maiden, fair, fascinating, full of smiles, compliments, and all sorts of winning ways, overflowing, moreover, with benevolence, and, therefore, prodigal to a fault in the language of praise. Nothing could be more fallacious than this mode of dealing with our question.

No, sir; flattery is far from being confined to slight

exaggeration, and innocent hyperbole, It is, in truth, a gigantic evil. It is interwoven with the whole framework of society, and encrusts it everywhere with the smooth shell of hypocrisy. Not only is the tongue enlisted in its service; but all features of the face, all motions of the body, are carefully trained to do its bidding. It is confined to no class; it is restricted to no country; it works always, and works stealthily; and, if unrestrained, would soon make us see, in a sense different from that intended by Shakspeare, that

> "All the world 's a stage,
> And all the men and women merely players."

Now, sir, in this fact, in this universal presence of flattery, I find an argument. The power of the flatterer for mischief, nay, sir, the necessary result of his action, is greater far than that of the slanderer, because he has a wider field of operation. The slanderer must work cautiously; he must balance, with skill, the probabilities of the case; he must, as the last speaker has observed, summon in council the faculties of the mind, before he can venture to act at all. He knows that detection will not only be fatal to his plot, but, also, fatal to *him*.

But the flatterer, confident of success, because he is confident of a pleasant reception, and because, moreover, he has, generally, no apprehension of personal danger, proceeds to his task without delay or impediment. If he succeed, his joy is complete; if he fail, he has suffered nothing but slight repulse,—a look of pity, or a smile of contempt.

The necessity of caution and the dread of consequences, you see, sir, seriously impede, and greatly circumscribe the operations of slander. Still further are they limited by the comparative fewness of the objects, upon which it can be made to operate at all. If appearances be not decidedly against the party slandered, or the ear of the listener be not strongly predisposed, the voice of the slanderer is heard usually with something of distrust. The semblance of truth must be carefully preserved in every particular; for the least improbability is sure

> "To cast
> Ominous conjecture on the whole success."

Flattery, on the other hand, courses, unchecked, over the whole field of human existence. It clothes the maiden with imaginary charms, and satisfies her soul with empty professions; it diverts the manly youth from sober pursuits, makes him impatient of salutary restraints, and absorbs his time in enervating pleasures; it dims the vision, and weakens the arm of parental discipline; it urges folly to claim the honor due only to wisdom; it induces cowardice to be perfectly content with the mere uniform of courage; in short, it encourages all the vices and defects of the race, to hide their native deformity, even from themselves, under the forms and coverings peculiar to the virtues and perfections opposite to each respectively.

If you ask for particular examples, they start up in every direction. Look at yonder rich man's table. Who is he, with servile look and mock delight, that sells his birth-right of independence for a mess of pottage? It is the parasite,—a name that contains the best history of the man.*

Who are these finely dressed, but anxious looking people, craving admission into the circles of the so-called aristocracy? They are those mistaken children of fashion, in whom flattery has contrived to extinguish all proper self-respect, and implanted, in its stead, a vain desire to be considered the *elite;* who, flattered by the condescensions of those whom they suppose to be above them, mistake sufferance for civility, and the form for the fact of high social standing.

But who is this? He is all graciousness,—"all things to all men," not, however, that he "may by all means, *save* some," but that he may, by *any* means, inveigle many. With what hearty grasp he seizes the hand of the sturdy smith! How eagerly he inquires after his family; how ready his joke, how loud his laugh! Was ever man so social? Who is he? The politician,—the keen pursuer of place and power. He is now a candidate for some lucrative office, and these people, among whom he is so freely dispensing bows, smiles and compliments, are the voters. What are his claims to preferment? His skill in the use of flattery.

What palace is this? It is the abode of the courtier—the professional flatterer. Let us enter. Who are these, with eager look and anxious brow, that await his coming in the spacious hall? It is the crowd of expectants, whom his reputed kindness and affluence have

* *Parasite,* (from the Greek παρά, *near,* or *beside,* and σῖτος, *food)* means, literally, one who takes food with another; thence it came to be applied to one who assents to, fawns upon, or servilely flatters another for the sake of food, or any other personal advantage.

attracted to his door. How graciously, at length, he enters the apartment! His smile, his nod, his whole demeanor, how inspiring to the heart of needy, hoping humanity! But heavy is the disappointment destined to succeed. There is no truth in him. It is the habit of his life,—the irresistible second nature that has fastened upon him, alternately to create and to destroy the hopes of his fellow men.

But yonder comes the conquering hero, heralded by the trumpet of fame,—that ingenious mouth-piece of flattery. How sweet to him is the sound of that trumpet! It drowns the groan of the dying, the wail of the widow, the maiden's lament and the orphan's cry. It stirs ambition, it fires the soul, and hides in romantic interest the horrors of the battle field. It tells of power, it tells of glory, not only to the present, but to future generations. How sweet is the sound of that trumpet! Alas! too often sweet, only because it feeds an insatiate and remorseless vanity.

But, Mr. President, I will not trouble you with further instances. Whichever way I look, I see the workings, or the sad results of the workings, of flattery; and whichever way I survey her movements, she appears as a two-edged sword, cutting keenly in both directions—the flatterer and the flattered. He that gives and he that takes this dangerous draught, are often equally and hopelessly wounded.

Much, much may we dread the tooth of Slander, but is not the tongue of Flattery still more dreadful?

SECOND DEBATE.

WHICH IS PREFERABLE, CITY OR COUNTRY LIFE?

FIRST SPEAKER.

Mr. President,—The question which we are now about to discuss,—"*Which is preferable, city or country life?*"—though apparently simple, is far from being devoid of difficulties. I have no hesitation, however, in declaring my preference for the country; though I deeply regret, that the limits to which I am here confined, utterly forbid any attempt to assign *all*, or any considerable *part* of my reasons for that preference. I must, indeed, content myself, for the present, with the statement of a single argument. It will be found, I hope, so impressive, because so *truthful*, that conviction must follow in its train.

I refer here to the argument derived from what I shall venture to call the *moral* influence of rural scenes. The country, sir, is the natural abode of man. There he is in constant communion with nature. There, undistracted by the tumults of trade, unenslaved by the tyranny of fashion, unpolluted by the vices of a promiscuous populace, he walks and works from day to day, amid mountains and valleys, meadows green, and cultivated fields, and all else that can inspire gratitude and devotion to the great Giver of all good.

There man has frequent opportunities, nay, *invitations*, so to speak, to look into his own heart,—to commune with his own spirit,—to develop and strengthen his native powers; in short, to train and discipline his whole physical, moral, and intellectual nature. If you would allow a man, unfettered, to become what he is capable of becoming, you must not throw him into the turmoil and bustle of towns and cities.

There he will, perchance, become what is called a "business man;" there he may become a *millionare;* there he may circulate freely in the gay assemblies of fashion; but there he cannot easily realize the true dignity of manhood. There is something in the very quiet and solitude of the country, which wonderfully elicits thought, develops character, and makes the *man*. Well has the poet said:—

"Where is the wise, or the learned, or the good that sought not solitude for thinking,
And from seclusion's secret vale brought forth his precious fruits?
Forests of Aricia, your deep shade mellowed Numa's wisdom;
Peaceful gardens of Vaucluse, ye nourished Petrarch's love;
Solitude made a Cincinnatus, ripening the hero and the patriot;
And taught De Stael self-knowledge, even in the damp Bastile;
It fostered the piety of Jerome, matured the labors of Augustine;
And gave imperial Charles religion for ambition;
That which Scipio praised, that which Alfred practiced,
Which fired Demosthenes to eloquence, and fed the mind of Milton,
Which quickened zeal, nurtured genius, found out the secret things of science,
Helped repentance, shamed folly, and comforted the good with peace,
By all men just and wise, by all things pure and perfect,
How truly, Solitude, art thou the fostering nurse of greatness!"

SECOND SPEAKER.

Mr. President,—The speech just delivered, (I mean no discourtesy,) is certainly not without merit, if considered merely as a picture of fancy. But, sir, *fancy* is not *fact;* and is, therefore, a very unfit material out of which to construct an argument. He says, that the dweller in the country is "in constant communion with nature": discerning, as it seems to me, no difference between *contact* and *communion.*

Country people are, indeed, in perpetual *contact* with those natural objects, which often awaken thought and foster devotion; but to infer from this, that they are actually always in sweet and sober *communion* with the beauties and sublimities of the scenery, amid which they dwell, is fanciful in the highest degree.

In reflecting upon rural life, we are very apt to fix our thoughts exclusively on grand and imposing features in nature,—on what is fair and beautiful, and fitted to excite pleasurable emotions, and to shut our eyes against its sterner and more repulsive aspects. Our imagination draws lively landscapes, and peoples them with souls of almost superhuman purity and innocence. It withdraws from the scene the digging and the delving, the bogs, the marshes, and all the nameless annoyances and hardships that constitute the stern realities of country life.

It calls into beings shepherds and shepherdesses, nay, rustics of every name and occupation, all gentle, all lovely, all kind, all uncontaminated by contact with vicious associations, and breathing a perfectly pure and healthy moral atmosphere. It, moreover, endows these people with peculiar tendencies to contemplation, makes them specially susceptible to the impressions of grand and noble scenes, and almost altogether free from the common propensities and waywardness of humanity.

Mr. President, such views of country life may befit those who supply the world with what is called, Pastoral Poetry; they may do to beguile a leisure hour, or feed a morbid imagination; but depend upon it, they have no *real* existence. Let any man mingle freely with country people; let him examine their habits, manners, their common, every-day life and conversation; and he will not be long in discovering, that the argument of the gentleman is wholly fallacious.

Allowing what you will for the influence of sublime and beautiful objects on the heart, it must be recollected that familiarity itself begets *indifference*, and that men soon come to walk among the Alps as among common hills, to sail over ocean billows as over the ripples of a quiet lake, and in short, to look, with comparative unconcern, upon things familiar, though they be the most thrilling and wonderful works of Creation.

The argument, therefore, which the gentleman has selected, with such apparent confidence in its force, is not, in my judgment, a conclusive one. It shows, it is true, that the country *offers* many features well *fitted* to awaken emotion and improve the heart; but it does not *prove* that these objects always produce that effect. I may, therefore, conclude by informing him, that his argument is just as true when applied to the city. The *city*, also, has many objects admirably adapted to arouse our better nature, and promote our spiritual well-being; but, alas, they are seldom, ay, very seldom, duly regarded.

THIRD SPEAKER.

Mr. President,—Instead of stopping to examine and refute what seems objectionable in the views expressed by the last speaker, I propose to introduce some two, or three new arguments, or considerations in favor of rural life. It will hardly be denied, that contact with *vice* has a corrupting influence, even by those who deny that contact with country scenes and objects, has no necessary improving power; for, "Evil communications," says an inspired writer, "corrupt good manners;" and this I hold to be true, whether in the city, or the country.

The only question is, which yields the *greater* amount of evil. Now, will any one deny this bad distinction to the city? And, if this be not denied, manifestly the country, on the score of morals, is the better, because the *safer* place.

But, again, sir, the country has a most decided advantage over the city, as a place for *intellectuul culture.*

It gives freedom from tumult, noise, and distracting excitements. It guaranties exemption from a thousand intrusions and interruptions, inseparable from city life; favors abstraction and concentration of the mental powers, and so secures to the student the best results of intellectual labor.

In proof of this, which is so clear in theory, I might

cite the testimony of experience—the experience of poets, orators, writers, and thinkers of every name and grade, and of almost every age and clime. But why dwell on a point so evident?

Again, the country favors not only mental and moral culture, but is eminently adapted to the *development of the physical constitution.* Every one knows, that city life, for the most part, is a thing altogether *artificial.* It cramps the feet with tight shoes, it compresses the waist with tight dresses; it invites and fosters colds, coughs, and consumptions, through the agency of thin stockings, light clothing, late hours, and many other similar requirements of fashion, which time would fail me to specify.

Nor is this all. The resident of the city not always enjoys the fresh products of the country, though he be ever so willing to *pay* for them. He must often be content with stale butter, stale milk, stale everything; while the happy farmer partakes of all these things in their freshness and purity. May we not, sir, in view of these and other kindred advantages connected with a residence in the country, may we not ask your decision in our favor?

FOURTH SPEAKER.

Mr. President,—From the observations of the gentleman who has just taken his seat, one might, without an appeal to facts, naturally infer, that all *good* is confined to the *country*, and all *evil* centered in the *city.* In the life of a citizen, he finds a sort of Siberian destitution; so that whether he walks, or talks, or studies, or eats, or drinks, or exercises, he is equally the victim of tyrannical custom.

Well, sir, to this doleful catalogue of imaginary ills, which must surely be regarded as the offspring of a distempered fancy, I can only append that old, familiar caption of certain newspaper paragraphs,—"Important, if *true*."

Why, sir, who ever heard, till this hour, that study was a thing to be done to the best advantage only "out in the country?" There only, it seems, we can get clear of noise and nuisance enough to enable us to think; as if people of studious habits, living in the city, were obliged by some unrelenting fatality to choose for a study just that spot in a town, where most "do congregate" carts, wagons, stages, and wheel-barrows, and where the din and clatter of commercial transactions are the most unceasing, and the most annoying; or, as if all parts of a city, and at all times of the day, were equally and hopelessly given up to clamor, uproar, and confusion.

Talk about opportunities for study? Where can they be *better*, where can they be as *good* as in the city? Here are capital schools, capital teachers, capital apparatus, capital libraries, capital courses of lectures, capital chances for literary conversation; in fact, capital chances for every thing that can enlarge, store, train, and liberalize the mind.

If we adopt the oft-reiterated sentiment, that

"The proper study of mankind is *man*."

and, for the prosecution of this study, seek the society of shade, and stream, and forest, and valley, where men are found few in numbers, and free from the excitements and conflicts, the competitions and vicissitudes that force out motive, and so determine the character of actions, we shall soon discover that our means of improvement, are sadly deficient. The city, sir, whatever our first impressions might suggest, is, without doubt, the best school for the study of the human heart; so that, if, indeed, "the proper *study* of mankind is man," the proper *place* for that study is the crowded city. "Glorious, indeed," says Longfellow, "is the world of God *around* us, but more glorious the world of God *within* us!" That "world of God *within* us," sir, which is destined to survive "the world of God *around* us," and which, for that reason, is the more deserving of our careful regard, is there best explored, where men, in masses, meet, jostle, rival and mutually stimulate one another.

But the gentleman dreads the vicious associations of the city. If that argument had any strength, it ought to drive him quite out of the world; for vicious people are, by no means, peculiar to cities. It ought, at least, to render him a hermit,—to force him into the most absolute asceticism; for nothing can be more obvious than, that vicious people are not the peculiar heritage and burden of cities.

Evil thrives, with more or less vigor and virulence, everywhere. We can not run entirely *away* from it, though we need not, and should not run heedlessly or designedly *into* it. Our positive duty is to oppose it, whether in ourselves or in others. "Resist the devil," says the apostle James, "and he will flee from you."

Surely, Sir, this Scriptural instruction differs *toto cœlo* from that which counsels us not to *resist*, but to *run.*

The truth is, Mr. President, there is often a positive advantage in being near to the wicked and the degraded, provided we have the heart to seek to do them good. Christ himself affords, by his practice in this regard, as in all others, the best possible example. He was found among the wicked, the outcast, the wretched: saying in answer to the question, "Why eateth your master with publicans and sinners?" "They that be whole need not a physician, but they that are sick." By following this divine example, sir, we may derive the highest benefit to ourselves, while we are seeking to alleviate the woes of others.

The spirit of true Christianity is no anchoretic spirit. It goes out among men, because evil is among men, and seeks, like its blessed Founder, "to save that which is lost." That wicked men, in numbers, dwell in cities, is therefore no argument to induce good men to flee to the country. It is rather a reason to make them court that trial of virtue, by which they may become at once the teachers and the taught in the ways and the works of God.

FIFTH SPEAKER.

Mr. President,—If I wished to give a distinct notion of the difference in signification, between the words *ingenious* and *ingenuous*, I think I might safely say, that, in this discussion, thus far the arguments *for* the country have been *ingenuous*, while the answers to them have been *ingenious.*

The country, says the first speaker, in substance, abounds in scenes and objects fitted to awaken admiration, and turn the thoughts of men toward their Creator. It differs from the city, in being the *natural*, instead of the *artificial* dwelling-place of man, and is, therefore, better adapted to the development of his mental and moral character.

Now, this is a plain and *ingenuous* statement of truth; powerful, indeed, but only powerful, because it is true. But how is it answered? "Oh," says the next speaker, "that's all *fancy!* Men soon become indifferent to the impressions of external grandeur. These things may be *fitted* to excite sublime sentiments and holy affections, but they seldom *do;* for men are apt to pass them by unheeded."

Then the whole argument is dismissed with a fine flourish of words about people walking among the Alps, as they would among common hills, and riding on the waves of the ocean as thoughtlessly as they would on the gently ruffled surface of a tranquil lake. In all this, the real point, on which the argument was obviously meant to turn, viz.: the *comparative* influence of city and country scenes and objects on man's moral nature, is quite overlooked. Now, sir, this may be considered *ingenious*, but it is far from being *ingenuous.*

Again; it was argued that the quiet and seclusion of rural life, afforded *better* opportunities for study and reflection than can be realized in the city; where there must be much of bustle and uproar,—the necessary concomitants of trade and commerce. In reply to this, we are rather tauntingly told, that people in the city, who are inclined to study, do not, for that purpose, seek those parts of the town most beset with the noise of carts, and the clamor of commerce.

And, as if to draw the mind entirely away from the point in debate, that is, from a simple *comparison* of advantages, where both places are admitted to have, at least, *some* claims to the thing in dispute, we are boastfully reminded, that in cities there are capital schools, capital lectures, and capital everything! Surely, sir, this is somewhat *ingenious* in the way of logic; but is it candid? Is it *ingenuous?*

It was further argued, that the country is comparatively free from the vicious associations that are always collected in large cities; and forthwith a gentleman tells us that evil exists everywhere, and then quotes Scripture to show what nobody denies, namely, that we must "resist the devil." This is another specimen of logical *ingenuity;* but it wants the very life and soul of logic, that is, the open and *ingenuous* spirit, that befits the investigation of truth.

Such, sir, is the reasoning, which has here been employed, in the attempt to invalidate the claims of the country to superior regard, as a place of residence. Vain attempt! "God made the country," some one has well observed, "but man made the city;" and there is here, as in all things else, the same measureless distance between the works of divinity and the works of humanity.

The city, sir, is a contrivance of trade,—trade that fosters "the love of money, which is the root of *all* evil,"—trade, that enslaves all the powers of the mind, and lashes them into the degrading service of Mammon,—trade, that tempts men to trickery and falsehood,—trade, that makes them hasten to be rich, and so "pierce themselves through with many sorrows."

The city, sir, is the convenience and theatre of fashion,—fashion that engenders fops and fools who delight in simulation and *dis*simulation; anxiously laboring to *seem* to be what they are *not*, and *not* to be what they *are*,—fashion, that forms and fosters hollow and deceitful friendships and alliances, makes happiness dependent upon the cut of a coat, the shape of a hat, the fit of a boot, or the length of a moustache, and resolves all gentility into a slavish conformity with modes of dress and *ad*dress, often absurd and ridiculous, and rarely convenient to nature.

The city is the nursery of social vice;—that vice, I mean, that can thrive only in the midst of multitudes; that shelters itself under the concealments of trade, and fashion, and politics, and whatever else may yield a fair outside, and so saps, unseen, the very foundations of virtue.

Why is it, sir, that people worn out, or disgusted with the toil and turmoil of trade, or with the empty and wearisome round of fashionable dissipation, or with the sorrowful vicissitudes of political ambition, fly away to the enchanting embrace of rural life, and seek in nature's path what was vainly, though eagerly, pursued amid the artificial arrangements and conventional restraints of city life? It is because the country, being agreeable to nature, furnishes just those means and modes of enjoyment, which are the most effective and permanent, because they are the most reliable.

There healthful labor brings its natural reward,—

"*a sound mind in a sound body.*" There the eye is gratified with scenes of beauty and sublimity; there the ear is delighted with the song of birds and all the melody of nature; and there, if we will, we may, in *truth*,—

"Look through nature up to Nature's God!"

SIXTH SPEAKER.

Mr. President,—I have no disposition to imitate the example of the last speaker, in complaining of the course taken by others in the debate; but I cannot resist the conviction, that the *real* point in dispute has not yet been fully brought out and discussed. I do not flatter myself, that *I* shall be able to do it, as it ought to be done. Yet, something in this way, I shall attempt.

The statement of the case, seems to be this. Two individuals, early in life, equal in health, fortune, and in social position, propose to themselves the question: "Which is *preferable*, city or country life?" It is not which would be preferable, supposing a man to be eager after wealth, or fashion, or some other specific object, which cities alone can confidently promise, because of the number and variety of the people in them; neither is it, which would be preferable, supposing a man to be in quest of health, or disgusted with the tedious and trifling ways of fashion, or worn out with the cares of business, or dejected and disheartened by the disappointments of ambition, or bent upon nothing but sober, profound, and protracted studies.

The question respects exclusively neither of these supposed conditions or characters; for, if it did, its decision would be easy. The claims of the city, for the one party, would be so absolute and overpowering, as to be quite irresistible; while the claims of the country, for the other party, would be no less cogent and convincing.

Now, with this, the true aspect of the case, that is *other things being equal*, "which is preferable, town or country?" I think I may assume a position in favor of the former, that cannot easily be controverted. I set out with the observation, that the town affords several advantages which cannot be had, nor compensated for, by a resort to the country. There is a certain polish and refinement acquired in city circles, or by the gentle attrition of city associations, whether for pleasure or business, which nothing in ordinary rural life, can either produce or atone for.

This has been experienced always and everywhere. The very words *civility*, from *civis*, in Latin, *a citizen; urbanity*, from *urbs*, *a city*, in the same language; and, as has been affirmed by some, *polite*, from the Greek *polis*, *a city;* these very words, I say, all expressive of that suavity and polish of manners that are essential to the true gentleman, show what has been the judgment of mankind for centuries, respecting the influence of cities upon human character.

A second peculiar advantage of living in a city, arises from the multiplicity and proximity of its means and appliances for comfort and convenience. Whoever has experienced the annoyances growing out of the privations of country life, in this respect, will need no lengthy argument to make him feel its force. In the country, days and even weeks of delay and consequent discomfort, spring from the want of things that every corner, in a city, offers in perpetual abundance.

In the country, with but few intervals of relief, a walk in the roads is but a weary wading through mud, or snow, or a ceaseless contact with clouds of dust. In the city, except under a weak and inefficient administration of the laws, well-paved streets and walks, and withal, well cleaned and sprinkled, invite the pedestrian to out-door business or exercise. Even at night, when the country is everywhere shrouded in robes of darkness, the city, all brilliant with lamps, along the streets, and in the countless shops and saloons, offers both pleasure and safety in walking abroad.

In the country, such is the temptation to impertinent curiosity, that everybody's business seems to be every *other* body's business, and all and each, like the Athenians of old, seem "to spend their time in nothing else, but either to tell, or to hear some new thing." In the city, every man has enough, and sometimes *more* than enough of his own business to attend to; and so it comes to pass, that whether one eats or drinks, whether he rides or walks, marries or is given in marriage, buys or sells, or whatsoever he does, that is legal and proper, arrests no special attention, and calls for no general talk or silly wonderment.

A third peculiar benefit, in city life, is impressively known and felt only when we are taken dangerously ill, or suddenly meet with some bodily calamity. In the country where the population is sparse, a single physician is all that can ordinarily be supported, in a widely-extended district.

It results, especially in cases of sudden and dangerous emergency, that the greatest delay and difficulty are experienced in securing timely medical aid and attendance. In the city, on the contrary, physicians and surgeons of all grades, are ever at hand, because, in cities alone, can they, in such numbers, be supported and encouraged. None can fail at once to see the singular superiority, in this respect, of the city over the country.

But, sir, I will pursue the subject no farther. I will not even claim the privilege, so freely accorded to others, that of calling to my aid the sweet voice of song. Rather let my arguments, whether worthy or worthless, stand all alone; unaffected by the magic influence of metre, the felicities of rhyme, or the airy forms of imagination.

I will only remind you, in conclusion, that the question should be decided on *general* grounds; that the respective claims of town and country are to be made upon those who are in a condition to *choose*, without the bias or necessity resulting from particular aims or personal and peculiar habits or infirmities.

And, judging in this, the only fair and philosophical manner, I claim for the city—that splendid result of human progress—that glorious achievement of associated labor and enterprise—that spacious field for the exercise of Christian virtues—that noble encourager of the arts and sciences—that matchless medium of trade and commerce—that wondrous combination of comfort and convenience—that incomparable nursery of the suavities and amenities of life, a true and triumphant decision in our favor.

SPEECH OF THE PRESIDENT.*

Gentlemen,—The debate, on the present occasion, though, in several respects, quite meritorious, exhibits, as it seems to me, several deficiencies deserving of notice. Some considerations, decidedly subordinate, have been injudiciously compelled to wear the aspect of weighty reasons; while arguments of real power, through some want of skill or care in directing their force, have either been kept in the back ground, or made altogether to miss their aim. Besides the end of all wise discussion,—*the elicitation of truth*, has not been, in my judgment, sufficiently kept in view. The spirit of the debate seems rather to have been the spirit of conquest.

I, therefore, propose, with your permission, to defer the duty of summing up and deciding, which devolves upon me, according to our rules, until the question has been more largely and liberally discussed; proposing,

* It is customary in some societies, after the debate, to leave the decision of the question to the judgment of the presiding officer. When such is the case, it is usual for him "to sum up," that is, to pass in review the principal arguments employed by the several speakers, compare them one with another, and so exhibit the grounds of his decision.

In the present instance, the President is made to defer his decision, and to take occasion, in its stead, to offer some suggestions respecting the mode of conducting a discussion. Such incidental hints or instructions a discreet presiding officer may often impart with great advantage.

for this purpose, that the debate be resumed at our next regular meeting. Meantime, allow me to occupy a few moments in venturing upon several suggestions and observations, designed, however feebly, to impart to the debates in this place a character more in harmony with the professed object of our Association, which is, you know, *the moral and intellectual improvement* of our own members.

I set out with this, as a prime rule of conduct in all debates,—that truth, and truth only, must be sought after, cherished and advocated; while error, whether in ourselves or in others, whatever sacrifice it may cost us, must be avoided, discarded, and condemned. This is a hard rule to work by; for such is the tenacity with which we cling to opinions and prejudices once entertained, that it is difficult to let them go, and more difficult still to confess, even by implication, that we have been wrong.

There is moreover, a certain love of victory, natural to the human heart, which finds nourishment in contests of all kinds, and which often tempts the unwary disputant "to make the worse appear the better reason," and so secure a triumph at the expense of truth. You can not, therefore, my friends, be too cautious, too resolute, or too self-denying, in the application of this rule.

This leads me to a second precept, closely allied to the first, namely, to enter into the discussion of a question, with a mind *prepared* to accept truth, because it *is* truth; no matter *who* presents it, or on what *side* it appears. Such a preparation, however, is not to be acquired without effort. It implies a relinquishment of all disposition to take unfair advantages.

It carefully excludes the spirit of perversion; tolerates none of those countless shifts and subtleties that officiously offer their services in the defense of error and prejudice; admits what is true as readily as it denies what is false; guards the speaker against the indulgence of petty personalities; teaches him to exercise every forbearance and every courtesy, but at all hazards, through whatever clouds of words, flashes of wit, assaults of satire, or thunder of oratory, to make his way steadily into the presence of all-enchanting all-satisfying truth.

A third rule of discussion is,—to study the subject of debate well beforehand, and, in so doing, take the widest and most liberal views; determining your position only after pondering deeply both sides of the question, and carefully measuring and comparing the forces of each respectively. And when once you have *chosen* your position, seek to fortify it in your own minds by an orderly and apt arrangement of all your arguments; so that when you come to be put upon the defense, you may have perfectly at command the whole of your resources.

This being done, have in readiness for detail and specification, those weak and untenable grounds which, by previous study, you have ascertained to be among the defenses of those who take the opposite side. This will command for you the respect that ever falls to him who is found to be acquainted with his theme, besides saving you the mortification of confessing ignorance and talking at a venture.

The fourth and last rule which time here allows me to offer, is,—ever to observe the rules of order and the courtesies of debate. "Order," it has been well said, "is Heaven's first law;" and nowhere, in the universe, is that law more indispensable than in a deliberative assembly.

Every speaker should feel himself under the strictest obligation to maintain in practice, as in precept, the rules and regulations adopted for the government and conduct of our meetings. Nor is this all. Above and beyond all the written requirements of the case, there is a certain educated refinement of manners,—a suavity of look, of word, and of act, without which all discussion savors of insolent contradiction, all debate sinks down into noisy wrangling.

He, then, who indulges much in the use of repartee, or satire, or ridicule, or whose deportment is so shaped as to wound the feelings of his opponent, thereby proves himself a practical enemy to the investigation of truth; since his conduct shuts up all the reliable avenues to conviction, turns the discussion into a contest of abusive utterances, and, instead of friendship, generates a brood of antipathies and resentments, that not only outlast the excitement of the occasion, but often go with us through all subsequent life. It is, therefore, impossible to be too strict in the observance of this last rule; for, in debating societies, as in all others, the precept of the Apostle is equally imperative, "Let all things be done DECENTLY and IN ORDER."

I forbear, Gentlemen, further to test your patience. I have no apology to offer for thus assuming to myself the office of an adviser; unless it can be found in the well-meant, if not well-considered, endeavor to advance the common interests of our Association.

SECTION XI.

DEBATES IN OUTLINE.

WHAT are here called Debates in Outline, are not, nor are they designed to be, elaborate synopses of all the arguments *pro* and *con*, that may be adduced in discussing the several questions proposed. They are to serve merely as *hints* and *suggestions*, as thoughts likely to beget thoughts.

He, therefore, that consults these outlines with any view to improvement, should consider their design, and act upon it. He should regard them not so much as arguments, as the sources of arguments: keeping always in mind, that what we ourselves excogitate, however humble, and however often thought of by others, is, for all the purposes of mental training, a thousand times more valuable than the best and the most brilliant arguments, if merely borrowed from other people.

Yet, reading and conversation are not, therefore, to be despised or neglected, as useless or injurious. The error to be avoided, is that of substituting reading and talking for the weightier matters of thinking and reasoning.

Can we reasonably indulge the hope of Universal Peace?

First Speaker. (*Affirmative*).—That war is unnecessary, and, therefore, unjustifiable, is a conviction which reflecting men will find it difficult to resist. Every fresh experience serves only to weaken our confidence in the arbitration of the sword, and strengthen that which we have in the decisions of reason. This renders the hope of universal peace quite a rational one.

Second Speaker. (*Negative.*)—Wars generally originate in causes inseparable from the character of human nature,—ambition and selfishness. As long as these last, there will be war and bloodshed. You must change the radical nature of man, therefore, before you can hope for universal peace.

Third Speaker. (*Affirmative.*)—It is the glory of Christianity, that it changes the heart of man; implanting therein, in place of the evil passions which we by nature inherit, or, by practice, too readily acquire, those qualities of heart and mind, which cannot, for a moment, tolerate the presence of war.

Fourth Speaker. (*Negative.*)—Experience shows that Christians do not scruple to go to war. Some of the fiercest and foulest contests have been carried on by Christians, and that, too, under the name of Christianity. Witness the Crusades.

Fifth Speaker. (*Affirmative.*)—What are often called *Christian* nations, said an acute and pious clergyman of New England, should rather be called *christened* nations. It is not the name and profession of Christ merely, that is to eradicate evil from the world, but the *true spirit* of his religion. That religion certainly promises the reign of universal peace. It is, therefore, reasonable to expect it.

Ought Emulation in Schools to be encouraged?

First Speaker. (*Affirmative.*)—People never put forth their best efforts without the stimulus of rivalry. There must be something to be gained, as also something to be lost, or all energy will be paralyzed. This is the experience of mankind, and it ought to have weight in our decision.

Second Speaker. (*Negative.*)—Emulation is the parent of antipathy. Its presence in schools is fraught with mischief. It defeats all attempts at cultivating the spirit of brotherhood, because it virtually sets one against another.

Third Speaker. (*Affirmative.*)—Rivalry, in a school, is not necessarily bitter and vindictive. It must be generous. It must be regarded and used as a healthful incentive. It may be perverted, but this should not lead to its entire disuse.

Fourth Speaker. (*Negative.*)—All rivalry presupposes, that some must be beaten. Few only can be rewarded as victors; the many must suffer, however diligent, or otherwise deserving, the mortifications of open defeat.

FIFTH SPEAKER. (*Affirmative.*)—The chances of success are equal, and, therefore, the unsuccessful have no right to complain. In the great world without, to which schools ought to be preparatory, rewards are perpetually made dependent upon the same conditions, and no one complains, or has a right to complain.

SIXTH SPEAKER (*Negative.*)—The chances of success are not equal, because there is no necessary equality of talent or genius in the competitors. The whole is arranged, as though every thing depended upon the industry and perseverance of the rival candidates; whereas the most laborious and persistent effort is often the least successful, because nature has denied the requisite measure of ability. The rivalry thus becomes the source of injustice, of bitter heartburnings and rancorous hostility.

Is Party Spirit productive of more Good than Evil?

FIRST SPEAKER (*Affirmative.*)—Experience has shown, that all men act better under close supervision, than when left to themselves. Party spirit generates watchfulness on both sides, and so keeps both sides close to the path of duty.

SECOND SPEAKER. (*Negative.*)—Party spirit withdraws the mind and heart from our common country and her best interests to place them on a particular party.

It makes us eager to carry personal and private measures, and forgetful of, or unjust to, the general well-being. It makes the chief concern to be, not how shall the whole country prosper, but how shall a party triumph?

THIRD SPEAKER. (*Affirmative.*)—It is well known, that, men long in power are apt to become haughty and oppressive, and that, unwatched, they will fall into many wrong practices. Party spirit, in such case, acts as a corrective. It takes unfit men out of office, and supplies their places with others more suitable. It thus operates, also as a warning to those who, in official station, are prone to oppression or injustice.

FOURTH SPEAKER. (*Negative.*)—Party spirit begets such rancor, as ought never to exist in one man's heart towards another. Under this influence, men will quarrel, fight and even kill one another, though citizens of the same city, and professedly loving the same country, and the same civil institutions.

FIFTH SPEAKER. (*Affirmative.*)—Party spirit may be rancorous, but that is true of the spirit that operates even in religious disputes. Shall all discussions in politics and religion, all parties and denominations cease, because men will sometimes quarrel about these things? Are not the disputes occasioned by party spirit, the means of turning men's minds upon political rights and privileges, which might otherwise be overlooked and lost?

SIXTH SPEAKER. (*Negative.*)—The spirit of party is

not to be confounded with, and mistaken for, the spirit of patriotism. It is strictly a selfish, not a benevolent spirit. It is an unscrupulous spirit. It is not ashamed to resort to falsehood to accomplish its ends. It is the spirit that results in urging men to slander their neighbors, in producing riots, in civil war and bloodshed.

SEVENTH SPEAKER. (*Affirmative.*)—Party spirit enables the poor, but honest man to get office, as well as the rich. It brings associated effort and means to bear, in such case, and so prevents that odious aristocracy of money, which is ever ready to show its haughty airs and oppressive domination.

EIGHTH SPEAKER. (*Negative.*)—Party spirit, instead of being the friend and supporter of the poor, but honest man, is, in general, the sadly misdirected agent of the worst men and the worst measures. It arrays citizen against citizen, and deters good men from becoming candidates for office, by the certain doom of being exposed, in their private characters, to every outrage and indignity which slander and malignity can conceive or execute. Many countries have already been ruined by this execrable spirit; and, in our own, its destructive tendencies are every day becoming more and more apparent.

Are Debating Societies more beneficial than injurious?

FIRST SPEAKER. (*Affirmative.*)—Whatever tends to unfold truth and explode error, is doubtless useful.

Debating societies, well managed, do this, and, therefore, justly claim to be always far more beneficial than injurious.

SECOND SPEAKER. (*Negative.*)—Debating Societies are usually composed of young persons, who are apt to treat the gravest and profoundest subjects in a light and superficial manner. In this way, minds not yet formed by study and reflection, are more likely to injure than to benefit one another.

THIRD SPEAKER. (*Affirmative.*)—There is no such thing as unmixed good in the world. If, therefore, you reject Debating Societies on the ground of their being liable to abuse, you may as well reject hundreds of other good things for the same reason. They invoke thought, lead to useful comparisons of ideas, and so strengthen the mind.

FOURTH SPEAKER. (*Negative.*)—They beget a disputatious spirit; making people delight not so much in the acquisition of knowledge and the discovery of truth, as in captious criticism, and in the pride of victory.

FIFTH SPEAKER. (*Affirmative.*)—Debating Societies encourage the disposition to reading and study, afford excellent opportunities for practice in extemporaneous speaking, place us in the way of wholesome criticism, and furnish the mind with a wide circle of ideas.

Have the Crusades proved more beneficial than injurious to mankind?

FIRST SPEAKER. (*Affirmative.*)—The first result of the Crusades was to break the chains of bondage, moral, mental, and political, which held in abject slavery, as it were, the nations of Europe. This they did, by discovering to the down-trodden and ignorant masses the secret of their own strength, and enriching their minds with knowledge, previously and otherwise inaccessible.

SECOND SPEAKER. (*Negative.*)—What we call the Crusades were nothing but those ferocious wars, waged in the name of religion, and often carried on in a spirit befitting savage marauders rather than the friends of the Cross. The ill effect of the Crusades upon the Christian religion itself, was incalculable: destroying confidence in the truth and purity of a faith, in the cause of which, professedly, such immoralities and barbarities were committed.

THIRD SPEAKER. (*Affirmative.*)—The origin or secret motive of the Crusades is not here in dispute. The spirit in which they were conducted, it is not our present business to consider or characterize. Bad or good, these belong not properly to the matter in hand. Have the Crusades *resulted* well, not had they a pure origin, is the question. They certainly revolutionized the institutions and customs of the day, disseminated information, gave unity of purpose to masses hitherto divided by distance and by feuds, and planted the seeds of civil liberty, which have come up in the shape of well-ordered and free states, and otherwise variously improved the condition of the world.

FOURTH SPEAKER. (*Negative.*)—The spirit of persecution generated or fostered by those wicked expeditions, which has since, in so many instances, displayed its terrible rage, is among the *results* of the crusades. If, therefore, we look exclusively at results, this one bad, horribly bad, consequence of them, ought to outweigh a score of those advantages commonly said to have come from them.

FIFTH SPEAKER. (*Affirmative.*)—No extensive reformation was ever made in any age, or country, that did carry with it the necessity of strong measures, and exhibit from the blindness and weakness of even good men, certain excesses deeply to be deplored. The career of Cromwell, though ultimately productive of inestimable benefits, was often marked by acts that his best friends must forever, and deeply regret.

SIXTH SPEAKER. (*Negative.*)—It is taken for granted, generally, that numberless benefits, moral, social and political, flowed from the Crusades, which cannot be shown to have had this origin. Besides, all these benefits might, could, and in due time, would, have been realized from the exercise of truly Christian virtues, without resort to barbarous wars.

Is there more of real than of imaginary evil in the world?

FIRST SPEAKER. *Affirmative.*)—All evil is real, whatever its source. But of that kind which is meant in this question, that is to say, evil created by causes really existent, and not merely imaginary, the amount is vastly greater than that which is the offspring of fancy. Hunger, cold, disease and the like realities, leave no parallel in the list of fancied adversities.

SECOND SPEAKER. (*Negative.*)—The terrors of imaginary calamity beset us from childhood to old age. Who can estimate the mental agonies of childhood, suffering under the absurd impression of ghosts hovering around a neighboring tomb, or graveyard or dwelling? What chilling terrors often shake the frames of older folks under the same delusive apprehensions?

THIRD SPEAKER. (*Affirmative.*)—The cases even of children, to say nothing of older people, affected by fear of spectres, are comparatively few. But the real sources of misery, those which reason cannot dispel, are legion.

FOURTH SPEAKER. (*Negative.*)—Apprehended evils are, perhaps, quite as numerous as any real ones. They are, moreover, all the more severe, as they are aggravated indefinitely by the same fertile faculty, that originates them. Fancy, unrestrained by reason, is the mother of endless despondent day-dreams, the prolific source of hypochondriac or maniacal hallucination; often the cause of incurable madness. What evil is comparable to the loss of reason?

Is a lie ever justifiable?

First Speaker. (*Affirmative.*)—A lie is a story told with the intention to deceive. The question, therefore, may be resolved into this,—*Is there any such thing as innocent deception?* It is innocent, when practiced merely for sport, or for the benefit of the party deceived; as, where a sick child that dreads medicine, is assured, that it is not medicine, but something else, or when a robber is diverted from his purpose, by a timely and ingenious falsehood.

Second Speaker. (*Negative.*)—There is no such thing as a "*timely falsehood*": all lying is untimely, because it is always, directly or indirectly, the fruitful source of mischief and misery. Telling lies, in order to induce children to perform a duty, is only teaching them indirectly to sacrifice truth to expediency. They will follow your example, and apply it to cases other than those of seeming necessity. You may sometimes ward off present evil, perhaps, by resort to falsehood; but the injury done to truth, in all such cases, is greater than that avoided by its violation.

Third Speaker. (*Affirmative.*)—May I not save my life, which is endangered by the assaultof a madman, by practicing a deception upon him? May I not cheer and solace a despondent patient, by exciting false, but flattering hopes? Shall I deny my correspondent the courtesy implied in the usual close of a letter—"*Your Obt. Servant, &c., &c.,*" merely because it is strictly a departure from truth? May not a general practice falsehood to deceive and embarrass his enemy? May not one who has fallen into the hands of savages, save himself from their ferocity, if necessary, by lying?

FOURTH SPEAKER. (*Negative.*)—It is easy to multiply cases, wherein lying would seem to be innocent, because it procures a benefit. But all such argumentation falls instantly to the ground, when you remember, that, whatever may be our ideas of expediency and inexpediency, of right and of wrong, the rule which God has established, in the case, is one that admits of no exceptions. There is no license to lie; for we may not do evil even that good may come.

Which is the more detrimental, to be too credulous or too suspicious?

FIRST SPEAKER. Credulity is the parent of serious evils in every department of life. It invites imposition, and brings the greater pain, because it is ever attended with the consciousness, that we are deceived by our own folly.

SECOND SPEAKER. Perpetual suspicion is perpetual terror. It were better to be often deceived by false appearances and promises, than to suffer the evil of frequently rejecting what is true and reliable, under the impression that deception lurks in everything.

THIRD SPEAKER. Suspicion saves a man of business from being ruined in his dealings. It throws continual safeguards around his transactions, while credulity exposes him at every turn to the wiles of sharpers.

FOURTH SPEAKER. Suspicion may often save a man from the wiles of sharpers, but just as often cuts him off from the intercourse and sympathy of honest men. It begets in the soul foul opinions of mankind, and is apt to make the man that harbors it, just what he deems other men to be. Credulity, on the other hand, takes kind and liberal views of humanity. It is one of the phases of charity—the spirit that "*thinketh* no evil."

FIFTH SPEAKER. Credulity is the greatest of all cheats. It cheats a man out of his understanding. It makes him see all things in the wrong light. It believes what is false, as readily as it receives what is true. It swallows the lie that is ruinous to a friend, as quickly as it takes in the truest statements against a malicious enemy. It confounds all the ordinary distinctions between what is probable and improbable. It ignores all just and safe discrimination.

SIXTH SPEAKER. Suspicion shuts out of the heart all that gives confidence. Now, confidence between man and man is the very foundation of society, the indispensable element of the social compact. Whatever weakens and disturbs this feeling, wars against the best interests of mankind. It divides friends, it excites antipathies, it deranges business, it dissolves the most tender and the most sacred connections and associations of every kind.

Is the miser more injurious to society than the spendthrift?

First Speaker. (*Affirmative.*)—*Miser* means *miserable, wretched.* The application of this name to a person of covetous disposition, sufficiently evinces the judgment of mankind respecting the influence of avarice. It makes a man mean and miserable. It is hardly possible, by any stretch of prodigality, to injure one's own moral nature to the extent created by the habitual exercise of covetous practices. "Covetousness is idolatry." This is Bible testimony. It has no god but money.

Second Speaker. (*Negative.*)—Does not the spendthrift, also, bring irreparable mischief on himself? When exhausted of his means, he is doubly poor; not only without money, but without the habits necessary to get and keep it. What must be his remorse, too, in such case, knowing that his wastefulness has brought him to want, when, had he been frugal, he would have had enough, and something, perchance, to spare, to relieve the necessities of others.

Third Speaker. (*Affirmative.*)—The miser is a voluntary pauper. He denies himself and his family the comforts of life, while he has money in abundance. He denies his children thorough educational training, and, by his example, inspires others with the love of money, which is "the root of all evil."

Fourth Speaker. (*Negative.*)—If the miser denies bread to his children by his penurious habits, the spendthrift does precisely the same thing by his extravagance. The doom of poverty settles equally on both. He not only dissipates his own private means, to an extent that cripples all proper business energy, but is among those who, by squandering capital, prevent those extensive commercial enterprises that tend so much to elevate and enrich a nation.

FIFTH SPEAKER. (*Affirmative.*)—The miser, in order to hoard, withdraws large sums from the circulation of a country. He thus prevents money from doing its appropriate work, and so diminishes the prosperity of a community.

SIXTH SPEAKER. (*Negative.*)—The tendency of the course of a spendthrift is evil in the extreme; because it seduces young people into habits of expense and recklessness, and is wholly at war with the spirit of industry and economy. It is all the more pernicious, because it disguises its wickedness under the name of generosity; and, under that plea, is not unfrequently guilty of the grossest injustice.

SEVENTH SPEAKER. (*Affirmative.*)—The habit of regarding money as the chief good, and as, in itself, a thing greatly to be sought after, is apt to generate a spirit of dishonesty. It not only makes men mean, but it makes them unjust. But, if it had no other ill effect, its tendency to make a few immensely rich, while the many are distressedly poor, renders it more dangerous to society than extravagance ever can be.

EIGHTH SPEAKER. (*Negative.*)—Nothing can be

made out of the argument, that avarice generates dishonesty, for prodigality is well known to do the same thing, only in a higher degree. How many persons, young and old, have been utterly ruined by yielding to the temptations to dishonesty, inspired by habits of extravagance! Both of these characters are worthy of all condemnation, but that of the spendthrift is the more injurious to society, because it wastes the rewards of industry, and offers a greater number and variety of temptations to the young and the thoughtless.

Are Theatres more beneficial than injurious?

FIRST SPEAKER. (*Affirmative.*)—Whatever exposes vice, and commends virtue, is undeniably a public benefit. This is the special office of the drama. It discovers the secret springs of wicked deeds, brings virtue out, at last, always triumphant, and so gives wholesome and impressive warning to those disposed to evil. It is, in short, a sort of school of morals.

SECOND SPEAKER. (*Negative.*)—If the office of the drama is to expose vice and commend virtue, it certainly has not been very true to its obligations. Plays, for the most part, abound in obscenities and profanities. They represent vicious characters, in colors so fascinating, that unreflecting people rather admire than condemn them.

If the theatre be considered a school of morality, the devil, as Dr. Dwight has observed, must have turned schoolmaster. The moral instructions of the stage, even when unexceptionable, both in principle and in language, fail of their effect, because not given in the right time, the right place, and under the right circumstances.

THIRD SPEAKER. (*Affirmative.*)—Whatever exceptions may be found or imagined, the general rule is, that the drama is decidedly in favor of sound morals. If the moral teachings of the theatre fail of their object, the fault lies not in the teaching, but in the dullness or perverseness of the pupils. We might as well take exception to the teachings of the pulpit, because so many turn a deaf ear to the voice of the preacher. It should be considered a great advantage in the theatre, that it attracts and teaches classes of people, whom the appointed agencies of the church seldom reach or affect.

FOURTH SPEAKER. (*Negative.*)—It is idle to talk of the moral tendencies of the stage, when it is quite notorious, that actors and actresses themselves, to say nothing whatever of the auditors, are, with few exceptions, not a little profligate in character. The plays, whether you regard the language, the sentiment, the dress, or other kindred circumstances, are often highly objectionable in point of delicacy and refinement. What must be the character and tendency of that teaching, which attracts and delights the vicious, and which exercises no corrective influence, either upon the players themselves, or those who habitually attend upon their performances?

Fifth Speaker. (*Affirmative.*)—The stage is confessedly beneficial in a literary point of view, whatever we say about its moral bearings. For justness of pronunciation, for true emphasis, for appropriate gestures, for all the graces of oratory, it stands pre-eminent. "Why is it," said a distinguished clergyman once to a great actor, "that you players are able to excel our profession in awakening and prolonging attention?" "It is," said the actor, "because we represent fiction as if it were truth, while you represent truth as if it were fiction!" The theatre is a school of oratory, and the excellence of its instructions is well attested by the fact, that extracts from plays are universally employed in schools and colleges, as the best exercises in elocution.

Sixth Speaker. (*Negative.*)—It is not true that the pronunciation of the player is always in accordance with the most approved standards. In the matter of emphasis, gesture, and whatever else may be used to aid in giving the true effect to a piece, it is not denied, that great actors take great pains. But, in general, it may be affirmed with entire truth, that the theatre affords very imperfect exhibitions of character. If Shakspeare's plays be excepted, few others will be found, which do not frequently represent vice and virtue in strange, improbable, and often impossible situations. In the acting, moreover, there is little, or nothing, true to our every-day experience.

Seventh Speaker. (*Affirmative.*)—Theatres are excellent means of amusement. They mingle what is useful, with what is entertaining, and, as people must have entertainment, the theatre becomes a great public benefit by affording it. In all countries some public entertainments have been found necessary. The Olympic and other games, &c., &c., sufficiently attest this.

EIGHTH SPEAKER. (*Negative.*)—A man's character may often be determined, in some measure, by the character of his amusements. Now, what are the amusements at the theatre? Are they such as good men,—such as people of the best and purest morals, can fully approve and patronize? Are they not notoriously, such in general, as bring together and entertain the vile, the ignorant, the abandoned?

NINTH SPEAKER. (*Affirmative.*)—The just objects and character of the legitimate drama are not to be confounded with everything in that form, presented on the stage. The theatre, properly managed, is everything that has been claimed for it in this debate, and more. It is, then, emphatically a good school; the players being good men and women, the plays being works of genius, abounding in all that is fitted to mend the heart, to improve the taste, to please the imagination, and to delight the eye and the ear, while the audience, refined, cultivated, or at least moral and respectable, meet and part, not only without injury, but with positive benefit. Can any one doubt the utility of such a theatre?

TENTH SPEAKER. (*Negative.*)—The point to be settled in this controversy is not what theatres *might* be, but what they *are*. As they now exist, and are managed, and must continue to be managed, in all likelihood, they are the sources of evil in many forms. What with the ill tendencies of the plays themselves, what with the ill influence on the players and their hearers, what with the late hours and feverish excitement which they necessitate, what with the bad associations they throw in the way of the young and the innocent, what with the drinking shops, the gaming tables, and other nameless snares and abominations therein and thereabout abounding, the theatre seems really incapable of producing any good result whatever.

SECTION XII.

QUESTIONS WITH REFERENCES.

HERE we introduce a series of questions, with references under each to authorities or sources of information. We have not thought it desirable to make these references numerous: the object being rather to afford *data* for the exercise of mind than to throw open volumes exhausting the subjects in dispute.

I.

OUGHT THE PRESS TO BE WITHOUT LEGAL RESTRICTION?

ENCYCLOPÆDIA AMERICANA,—Article, "BOOKS, CENSORSHIP OF."
MILTON on the Liberty of the Press.
HUME's Essay on the Liberty of the Press.
COLERIDGE,—The Friend. Essay XXI.
DWIGHT'S Decisions.

II.

ARE FICTITIOUS WRITINGS MORE BENEFICIAL THAN INJURIOUS?

DUNLOP'S History of Fiction, from the earliest Greek Romances to the Novels of the Present Day.
WALTER SCOTT'S Criticism on Novels and Romances.
AKENSIDE'S Pleasures of the Imagination.
GOLDSMITH'S Citizen of the World,—Letter LIII.
MURRAY'S Morality of Fiction, or an Inquiry into the Tendency of Fictitious Narratives.

III.

DO SPECTRES, OR GHOSTS APPEAR?

PENNY CYCLOPÆDIA,—Article, "APPARITION."
WALTER SCOTT'S Demonology and Witchcraft.
HIBBERT'S Philosophy of Apparitions.
DWIGHT'S Decisions.
THACHER'S Essay on Demonology, Apparitions, and Popular Superstitions.
UPHAM'S Lectures on Salem Witchcraft.
NEWNHAM'S Essay on Superstition.
DEFOE'S History of Apparitions.

IV.

WAS THE BANISHMENT OF NAPOLEON TO ST. HELENA JUSTIFIABLE?

ALISON'S History of Europe.
THIERS' History of the French Empire.
O'MEARA'S Napoleon in Exile.
SCOTT'S Life of Napoleon.
ABBOTT'S Life of Napoleon.
HAZLITT'S Life of Napoleon.
MONTHOLON'S History of the Captivity of Napoleon at St. Helena.
BOURRIENNE'S Memoirs of Napoleon Bonaparte.

V.

IS WAR JUSTIFIABLE?

CHALMERS on the Hatefulness of War.
CHANNING on War.
JAY'S War and Peace.
WAR Inconsistent with the Religion of Jesus Christ, (New York 1815.)
DWIGHT'S Decisions.

VI.

OUGHT CLASSICAL STUDIES TO BE ENCOURAGED?

LOCKE'S Thoughts on Education.
ROBERT HALL on Classical Learning.
WHEWELL'S University Education.
SEARS, EDWARDS and FELTON on Classical Studies.
DONALDSON'S New Cratylus,—Introductory Chapter.
DWIGHT'S Decisions.
ARNOLD'S Miscellaneous Writings,—Article, "RUGBY SCHOOL."

VII.

DOES GEOLOGY CONFIRM THE MOSAIC ACCOUNT OF THE CREATION?

LYELL'S Principles of Geology.

HITCHCOCK'S Religion of Geology.

BUCKLAND'S Geology and Mineralogy.

WOOD'S Mosaic History of the Creation, illustrated from the Present State of Science.

TAYLER LEWIS' Six Days of Creation.

IRA HILL'S Theory of the Formation of the Earth.

"THE TWO RECORDS—THE MOSAIC AND THE GEOLOGICAL;" a Lecture delivered before the Young Men's Christian Association, in Exeter Hall, London.

VIII.

IS THE STUDY OF MYTHOLOGY MORE ADVANTAGEOUS THAN HURTFUL?

KEIGHTLEY'S Mythology.

DWIGHT'S Grecian and Roman Mythology.

BRYANT'S Analysis of Ancient Mythology.

SIR WILLIAM JONES on the Gods of Greece, Italy and India.

IX.

WAS THE FEUDAL SYSTEM BENEFICIAL?

PENNY CYCLOPÆDIA; also, BRANDE'S ENCYCLOPÆDIA OF SCIENCE, LITERATURE, AND ARTS,—Article, "FEUDAL SYSTEM."

HALLAM'S State of Europe during the Middle Ages.

BERINGTON'S Literary History of the Middle Ages.

X.

IS THE SENTIMENT—

"For forms of government let fools contest;
What 's best administered, is best"—

JUSTIFIABLE?

ENCYCLOPÆDIA AMERICANA,—Article, "NATURAL LAW."

ALGERNON SIDNEY'S Discourses on Government.

MONTESQUIEU'S Spirit of Laws.

CARLYLE'S Chartism.

ADAMS' Defense of the Constitution of the United States.

DE TOCQUEVILLE'S Democracy in America.

AUSTIN'S Constitutional Republicanism in Opposition to Fallacious Federalism.

XI.

ARE CRITICAL REVIEWS ADVANTAGEOUS TO SCIENCE AND LITERATURE?

ENCYCLOPÆDIA AMERICANA,—Article, "REVIEWS."
COLERIDGE'S Biog. Literaria,—Chap. XXI.
BYRON'S British Bards and Scotch Reviewers.
DWIGHT'S Decisions.
MARGARET S. FULLER'S Short Essay on Critics.

XII.

IS PHRENOLOGY ENTITLED TO THE RANK OF A TRUE SCIENCE?

SPURZHEIM'S Examination of Objections to Phrenology.
COMBE'S Elements of Phrenology.
JOURNAL of the London Phrenological Society.
AMERICAN Phrenological Journal.
REESE'S Phrenology known by its Fruits.
CALDWELL'S Phrenology Vindicated, and Anti-Phrenology Unmasked.

XIII.

IS THE MAXIM, "A POET IS BORN SUCH, NOT MADE," TRUE?

ENCYCLOPÆDIA BRITANNICA,—Article, "POETRY."
ROBERT HALL on Poetic Genius.
MACAULAY'S Essay on Milton.—Modern British Essayists, Vol. I.
JOHNSON'S Rasselas,—Chap.
JEFFREY'S Review of Campbell's Specimens of British Poets.—Modern British Essayists, Vol. VI.

XIV.

CAN THE EXISTENCE AND ATTRIBUTES OF THE SUPREME BEING BE DEDUCED FROM THE LIGHT OF NATURE?

CUDWORTH'S Intellectual System of the Universe.
PALEY'S Natural Theology.
BRIDGEWATER Treatises.
STURM'S Reflections on the Being and Attributes of God.
PLATO against the Atheists; or the Tenth Book of the Dialogue on Laws. By TAYLER LEWIS, LL.D.

XV.

IS CAPITAL PUNISHMENT JUSTIFIABLE?

ENCYCLOPÆDIA AMERICANA,—Article, "DEATH, PUNISHMENT OF."
SPEAR'S Essays on the Punishment of Death.
EDINBURGH REVIEW, Vol. XXXV., p. 320.
DWIGHT'S Decisions.
CHEEVER'S Defense of Capital Punishment, and LEWIS' Essay on the Ground and Reason of Punishment.
BRADFORD'S Inquiry on the Punishment of Death in Pennsylvania.
SULLIVAN'S Report to the Legislature of New York on Capital Punishment.

XVI.

WAS THE EXECUTION OF MARY QUEEN OF SCOTS JUSTIFIABLE?

ROBERTSON'S History of Scotland.
HUME'S History of England.
BELL'S Life of Mary.
ABBOTT'S Life of Mary Queen of Scots.
TYTLER'S Historical and Critical Inquiry into the Evidence produced against Mary Queen of Scots.
WHITAKER'S Vindication of Mary Queen of Scots.

XVII.

IS THERE A STANDARD OF TASTE?

BLAIR'S Lectures on Rhetoric.
KAMES' Elements of Criticism.
ALISON on the Nature and Principles of Taste.
MACKENZIE'S Theory of Taste.
M'DERMOTT'S Dissertation on Taste.
GERARD'S Essay on Taste.

XVIII.

IS THERE MORE TO APPROVE THAN CONDEMN IN THE CHARACTER OF OLIVER CROMWELL?

CARLYLE'S Letters and Speeches of Oliver Cromwell.
SOUTHEY'S Life of Cromwell.
HUME'S History of England.
CLARENDON'S History of the Rebellion.
NOBLE'S Memoirs of the Cromwell Family.
WALTER SCOTT'S Tales of a Grandfather.
GODWIN'S History of the Commonwealth of England.

XIX.

WHICH WAS THE GREATER POET, HOMER OR MILTON?

ADDISON'S Papers on the Paradise Lost, in the Spectator.

BLAIR'S Lectures on Rhetoric.

COLERIDGE on the Study of the Greek Poets.

THIRWALL'S History of Greece, Vol. I.

POPE'S Preface to his Translation of the Iliad.

XX.

ARE THE MENTAL FACULTIES OF THE SEXES EQUAL?

WALKER'S Woman Physiologically Considered, as to Mind, Morals, &c.

REV. SIDNEY SMITH'S Essay on Female Education—Modern British Essayists, Vol. III.

MRS. JAMESON'S Characteristics of Women, Moral, Poetical, Historical.

AIME' MARTIN'S Education of Mothers; Translated by EDWIN LEE.

FOREIGN QUARTERLY REVIEW, No. XXXIII,—Article II.

WESTMINSTER REVIEW, No. LXVIII,—Article II.

DWIGHT'S Decisions.

MARGARET S. FULLER'S Woman in the Nineteenth Century.

MARIA CHILD'S History of Women.

STARLING'S Noble Deeds of Women, or Examples of Female Courage and Virtue.

XXI.

IS THE PREVAILING SYSTEM OF EDUCATION FOR FEMALES WORTHY OF ENCOURAGEMENT?

HANNAH MORE'S Accomplished Lady, or Strictures on the Modern System of Female Education.

REV. SIDNEY SMITH'S Essay on Female Education.—Modern British Essayists, Vol. III.

FENELON on the Education of a Daughter.

MRS. SIGOURNEY'S Letters to Young Ladies.

MISS SEDGWICK'S Means and Ends, or Self-Training.

XXII.

IS THERE SUFFICIENT REASON FOR A BELIEF IN THE NATIONAL RESTORATION OF THE JEWS.

MILLMAN'S History of the Jews.

CUNNINGHAM'S Letters and Essays on Subjects connected with the Conversion and Restoration of the Jews.

BICHENO'S Restoration of the Jews, the Crisis of all Nations.

XXIII.

OUGHT SECRET SOCIETIES TO BE TOLERATED?

ROBINSON'S Proofs of a Conspiracy against all the Religions and Governments of Europe, carried on by Free Masons, Illuminati, and Reading Societies.

ARNOLD'S Philosophical History of Free Masonry, and other Secret Societies.

ENCYCLOPÆDIA AMERICANA,—Articles, "JESUITS, OR SOCIETY OF JESUS," and "JESUITS, written by a Jesuit."

STONE'S Letters on Masonry and Anti-Masonry.

LAWRIE'S History of Free Masonry.

SECRET SOCIETIES of the Middle Ages; (in the Library of Entertaining Knowledge.)

XXIV.

ARE BANKS MORE USEFUL THAN INJURIOUS TO A COMMUNITY?

TUCKER'S Theory of Money and Banks Investigated

GILBERT'S History and Principles of Banking.

LOGAN'S Popular Exposition of the Practice of Banking in Scotland.

LAWSON'S History of Banking. Revised, with numerous additions, by J. SMITH HOMANS.

FRANCIS' History of the Bank of England.

CLARKE'S History of the Bank of the United States.

WESTMINSTER REVIEW, No. LXVIII,—Article IV.

XXV

OUGHT THE PROTECTIVE POLICY OR FREE TRADE PRINCIPLES TO PREVAIL?

ADAM SMITH'S Wealth of Nations.

FOREIGN QUARTERLY REVIEW, No. XXIX,—Article I.

BASTIAT'S Sophisms of the Protective Policy.

RAGUET'S Principles of Free Trade.

LONDON QUARTERLY REVIEW, No. CXXXV,—Article VII.

RAE'S New Principles of Political Economy in Refutation of Adam Smith's Wealth of Nations.

BLACKWOOD'S MAGAZINE, No. CCCXLI, for March, 1844,—Article, "CORN LAWS."

RICARDO'S Principles of Political Economy and Taxation.

WAYLAND'S Elements of Political Economy.

XXVI.

IS THERE A POSSIBILITY OF REACHING THE NORTH POLE?

ENCYCLOPÆDIA AMERICANA,—Article, "NORTH POLAR EXPEDITIONS."

BARROW'S Chronological History of Voyages into the Arctic Regions, from the Earliest Period to Captain Ross' First Voyage.

ROSS' Arctic Voyages.

BARRINGTON'S Possibility of Approaching the North Pole Asserted, with papers on the Northwest Passage, by Col. BEAUFOY.

PARRY'S Three Voyages for the Discovery of the North-West Passage.

SIR JOHN FRANKLIN'S Arctic Expeditions.

KANE'S Arctic Expedition.

ARCTIC REGIONS, being an account of the Exploring Expeditions of Ross, Franklin, Parry, Back, M'Clure, and others, with the English and American Expeditions in search of Sir John Franklin (published by Miller, Orton, and Mulligan).

XXVII.

IS EMULATION A WHOLESOME STIMULANT IN EDUCATION?

HOBBES on Envy and Emulation.

COWPER'S Tirocinium.

DWIGHT'S Decisions.

EDGEWORTH'S Practical Education.

GODWIN'S Reflections on Education, Manners, and Literature.

XXVIII.

WAS THE EXECUTION OF MAJOR ANDRE JUSTIFIABLE?

ENCYCLOPÆDIA AMERICANA,—Article, "BENEDICT ARNOLD."

BENSON'S Vindication of the Captors of Major André.

SMITH'S Authentic Narrative of the Causes which led to the Death of Major André.

MISS SEWARD'S Monody on the Death of Major André.

XXIX.

HAS THE AUTHOR OF JUNIUS EVER BEEN IDENTIFIED?

ENCYCLOPÆDIA AMERICANA,—Article, "JUNIUS."

BRITTON'S Authorship of the Letters of Junius Elucidated.

JUNIUS Identified with a Distinguished Living Character, (N. Y., 1818.)

JUNIUS Unmasked, or Lord Sackville proved to be the Author of Junius, (Boston, 1828.)

XXX.

WOULD THE UNIVERSAL PREVALENCE OF SOCIALISM ADVANCE THE INTERESTS OF HUMANITY?

ROUSSEAU'S Inquiry into the Social Contract.
FISHER'S Examination of Owen's New System of Society.
CONSIDERATIONS of some Recent Social Theories (Boston, 1853).
LONDON QUARTERLY REVIEW, No. CXXX,—Article VI. (ON SOCIALISM).
BLACKWOOD'S MAGAZINE, No. CCCXLIX., for November, 1844,—
Article, "FRENCH SOCIALISTS."

XXXI.

ARE THE MODERNS SUPERIOR TO THE ANCIENTS IN RHETORICAL SCIENCE?

ARISTOTLE'S Rhetoric, translated by GILLIES.
CICERO De Oratore, translated by GUTHRIE.
QUINCTILIAN'S Institutes of Eloquence, translated by GUTHRIE.
LONGINUS on the Sublime, translated by W. SMITH.
DIALOGUE on Eloquence, attributed to TACITUS, translated by MURPHY.
HORACE De Arte Poetica, translated by P. FRANCIS.
CAMPBELL'S Philosophy of Rhetoric.
KAMES' Elements of Criticism.
WHATELY'S Rhetoric.

XXXII.

IS GENIUS INNATE?

BROWN'S Lectures on the Philosophy of the Human Mind.
REID'S Inquiry into the Human Mind.
LOCKE on the Human Understanding.
SHARPE'S Dissertation on Genius.
WHIPPLE'S Lecture on Genius.
BLAIR'S Lectures on Rhetoric.

XXXIII.

IS THE STORY OF THE TROJAN WAR CREDIBLE?

THIRWALL'S History of Greece.
LE CHEVALIER'S Description of the Plain of Troy.
BRYANT'S Dissertation concerning the War of Troy.
CHANDLER'S History of Ilium, or Troy.
GELL'S Topography of Troy.
WOOD'S Essay on the Genius and Writings of Homer.

XXXIV.

ARE NEGROES INFERIOR TO WHITE PEOPLE IN MENTAL CAPACITY?

PENNY CYCLOPÆDIA,—Article, "MAN."

GREGOIRE'S Inquiry Concerning the Intellectual and Moral Faculties of Negroes.

BRANDE'S Dictionary of Science, Literature, and Art,—Article, "NEGROES."

PRICHARD'S Researches into the Physical History of Mankind.

LAWRENCE'S Lectures on the Comparative Anatomy, Zoology, and the Natural History of Man.

COMBE'S Constitution of Man Considered.

ENCYCLOPÆDIA AMERICANA,—Article, "AFRICA."

XXXV.

IS THE CHARACTER OF QUEEN ELIZABETH WORTHY TO BE ADMIRED?

HUME'S History of England

AGNES STRICKLAND'S Queens of England.

SHARON TURNER'S History of England during the Reign of Edward VI., Mary, and Elizabeth.

LUCY AIKIN'S Memoirs of the Court of Queen Elizabeth.

ABBOTT'S Life of Elizabeth.

XXXVI.

IS THE STATEMENT,—"EVERY MAN IS THE ARCHITECT OF HIS OWN FORTUNE," TRUE?

DAVENPORT'S Lives of Individuals who have raised themselves from Poverty to Eminence and Fortune.

EDWARDS' Biography of Self-Taught Men.

MIDDLETON'S Life of Cicero.

HUGH MILLER'S My Schools and Schoolmasters.

PURSUIT of Knowledge under Difficulties, (published by the Harpers.)

BOYHOOD of Great Men; also, Footprints of Famous Men, (published by the Harpers.)

PARTON'S Life of Horace Greeley.

CARLYLE'S Review of Heeren's Life of Heyne,—Foreign Review, No. IV., 1828.

XXXVII.

WAS THE HARTFORD CONVENTION JUSTIFIABLE?

DWIGHT'S History of the Hartford Convention.

OTIS' Letters in Defense of the Hartford Convention.

XXXVIII.

ARE NOT THE VIRTUES OF THE PURITANS GENERALLY OVER-ESTIMATED?

NEAL'S History of the Puritans.

GREY'S Examination of Neal on the Puritans.

MADOX'S Vindication of the Church of England against Neal's History of the Puritans.

STOUGHTON'S Heroes of Puritan Times, with an Introductory Letter by JOEL HAWES, D.D.

YOUNG'S Chronicles of the Pilgrim Fathers.

XXXIX.

WAS THE EXECUTION OF CHARLES THE FIRST JUSTIFIABLE?

HUME'S History of England.

CLARENDON'S History of the Rebellion.

GUIZOT'S History of the English Revolution in 1640, from the Accession of Charles I. to his Death; translated by W. HAZLITT.

HALLAM'S Constitutional History of England; also, MACAULAY'S Review of the same (in Modern British Essayists, Vol. I.)

ABBOTT'S History of Charles I.

LUCY AIKIN'S Memoirs of the Court of King Charles I.

COURT and Times of Charles I. (London, 1848).

WESTMINSTER REVIEW, No. XLIII,—Article II.

XL.

IS THE EARLY LEGEND OF ROMULUS AND THE FOUNDATION OF ROME ENTITLED TO CREDENCE?

PLUTARCH'S Life of Romulus.

PENNY CYCLOPÆDIA,—Article, "ROMULUS."

ANTHON'S CLASSICAL DICTIONARY,—Articles, "ROMA" and "ROMULUS."

ABBOTT'S Life of Romulus.

NIEBUHR'S History of Rome.

ARNOLD'S History of Rome.

SECTION XIII.

MISCELLANEOUS QUESTIONS FOR DISCUSSION.

IN order to supply, in some degree, the demand for variety in the questions proper for discussion in Debating Societies, we append the following list, which contains, among many others, those, also, that have been used in the three sections preceding.

1. Ought the State to provide for the free education of all children within its borders?
2. Is a life of celibacy preferable to that of the married state?
3. Ought old Bachelors to be subjected to civil disabilities?
4. Should monopolies in trade ever be allowed?
5. Which yields the greater pleasure, anticipation or possession?
6. Is the maxim, "A poet is *born* such, not *made*," strictly true?
7. Ought ministers of the gospel to engage in party politics?
8. Which life is subjected to the greater hardship, the soldier's or that of the sailor?
9. Are the ancient Seres identical with the modern Chinese?
10. Ought there to be a law of international copyright?
11. Which contributes the more to eloquence, art or nature?
12. Ought the Protective Policy or Free-Trade Principles to prevail?
13. Which yields the higher entertainment, poetry or history?
14. Is it expedient to form colonies of convicts?
15. Is universal suffrage expedient?
16. Is the doctrine of human perfectibility true?

17. Can the immortality of the soul be proved from the light of nature alone?

18. Can a man who has been unjustly condemned to death, innocently withdraw himself from the hands of the law?

19. Ought gambling to be suppressed by law?

20. Do men suffer more, in this life, from real than from imaginary evils?

21. Ought a breach of promise of marriage to be punished merely by pecuniary fines?

22. Which abounds the more in sublimity, ancient or modern poetry?

23. Which exercises the greater influence upon mankind, hope or fear?

24. Which is the more serviceable to mankind, gold or iron?

25. Which is better for the development of character, poverty or riches?

26. Which is the better source of knowledge, reading or observation?

27. Ought the blacks of the free States to have the privilege of voting?

28. Is Roman Catholicism compatible with free institutions?

29. Would a repeal of the union between Ireland and England be beneficial to the former?

30. Would a large standing army be conducive to our country's prosperity?

31. Would a Congress of nations be practical or beneficial?

32. Were the Puritans justified in their treatment of the North American Indians?

33. Ought the liberty of the press to be restricted?

34. Was the Mexican war justifiable?

35. Has the Negro more ground for complaint than the Indian?

36. Was the banishment of Roger Williams justifiable?

37. Was Governor Dorr's imprisonment justifiable?

38. Was the war between England and China justifiable on the part of England?

39. Is England likely ever to become a republic?

40. Is the Wilmot proviso constitutional?

41. Ought our government to favor the building of a Pacific railroad?

42. Was the intervention of the French at Rome just and expedient?

43. Ought imprisonment for debt to be abolished?

44. Ought any foreign power to interfere in the affairs of Poland?

45. Ought religious institutions to be supported by law?

46. Were the Allied Powers justifiable in interfering in the affairs of Greece?

47. Was the field of eloquence among the ancients superior to that among the moderns?

48. Is Infidelity on the increase?

49. Is too high regard paid to antiquity?

50. Is there any limit to the progress of social improvement?

51. Ought the support of the poor to be provided for by the government?

52. Has the introduction of Christianity been unfavorable to poetry?

53. Ought the general government, or any state government, to compel all or any of the free blacks to remove to Liberia?

54. Are fictitious writings more beneficial than injurious?

55. Is assassination of tyrants justifiable?

56. Ought general governments to be invested with more authority?

57. Have European commotions a tendency to promote liberty

58. Ought Free-Masonry to be suppressed by law?

59. Is a public preferable to a private education?

60. Was the Hartford Convention justifiable?

61. Should the United States government have assisted in the emancipation of the Greeks?

62. Ought privateering to be allowed?

63. Ought lotteries to be tolerated?

64. Ought the Chief Magistrate of the Union to have the power to pardon criminals?

65. Ought infidel publications to be prohibited by law?

66. Are public executions preferable to private?

67. Ought a student to pursue professional studies, while in college?

68. Is rotation in office politic?

69. Do ghosts or spectres appear?

70. Is it politic for Universities in the United States to import their professors?

71. Ought the United States to encourage the Indians, now within their own limits, to emigrate further west?

72. Has the British Government in India been beneficial to the natives?

73. Have men of thought been more beneficial to the world than men of action?

74. Does the prevailing system of popular lectures in the principal cities of the country deserve our support?

75. Is the power of England beneficial to the world?

76. Are the principles of the Peace Society worthy of our support?

77. Which was the greatest historian, Hume, Gibbon, or Niebuhr?

78. Should the course of study in academies and colleges be the same for all the pupils?

79. Is it expedient to unite manual with mental labor in an educational establishment?

80. Are all mankind descended from one pair?

81. Is asceticism favorable to the development of Christian character?

82. Is it expedient to abolish the system of college commons?

83. Is not the production of such a poem as the Iliad incompatible with the idea of the supposed general ignorance prevalent in Homer's time?

84. Which is preferable, a sanguine, or a phlegmatic temperament?

85. Is childhood the happiest period of human life?

86. Were the Pelasgi and the Hellenes one in language and in origin?

87. Is not undue importance attached to precedents in our courts of law?

88. Has history been improved by the rejection of fictitious orations?

89. Which are the more praiseworthy, the Greek or the Roman historians?

90. Which was the greater poet, Milton or Homer?

91. Is poetical genius greatly benefited by extensive reading?

92. Is it unimportant what one's *doctrines* may be, so long as his *life* is in the right?

93. Are critical reviews advantageous to science and literature?

94. Which affords the better field for eloquence, the pulpit or the bar?

95. Is it judicious to read on a given theme before we write upon it in full?

96. Which exercises the greater influence on the character of the young, the teacher or the preacher?

97. Are the inequalities of rank and condition in society favorable to the advancement of learning?

98. Should an author rest his fame on few or on many books?

99. Ought public opinion to be regarded as the standard of right?

100. Was Bonaparte greater in the field than in the cabinet?

101. Is the savage state preferable to the civilized?

102. Are lawyers beneficial?

103. Ought the Judiciary to be independent?

104. Does temptation lessen the baseness of crime?

105. Can the existence and attributes of the Deity be proved by the light of nature?

106. Are Negroes inferior to white people in mental capacity?

107. Is a promise to a highwayman, not to take measures for his detection on the condition of sparing one's life, binding?

108. Are women more revengeful than men?

109. Is a mind of acute sensibility, on the whole, desirable?

110. Which is the more conducive to the best interests of the State, commerce or agriculture?

111. Ought persons differing in religious sentiment to be united in marriage?

112. Ought a Christian to unite in marriage with an unbeliever?

113. Is immersion essential to the validity of Christian baptism?

114. Is the maxim, "*No church without a bishop*," true?

115. Are the moderns superior to the ancients in poetry and eloquence?

116. Ought theological seminaries to be encouraged?

117. Is the assertion in the Declaration of Independence, "*that all men are created equal*," true?

118. Has the moral influence of the United States, on the whole, been salutary to the world?

119. Ought a man to pledge himself to total abstinence?

120. Has a man a right to kill another in self-defense?

121. Was the fate of Sir Walter Raleigh a deserved one?

122. Is the sentiment,—

> "For forms of government let fools contest;
> What 's best administered, is best,"—

justifiable.

123. Which exhibits the greater wonders, the land or the sea?

124. Ought human physiology to be a regular study in our common schools?

125 Is the doctrine of original sin taught in the Bible?

126. Has the Smithsonian Fund been employed in a manner accordant with the intention of the donor?

127. Would the universal prevalence of Socialism advance the interests of humanity?

128. Is morality separable from religion?

129. Ought normal schools to be supported by the State?

130. Is there Scripture authority for a belief in the Second Advent, and personal reign of Christ on the earth?

131. Ought not a bank of the United States to be reëstablished?

132. Is not the practice of auricular confession enjoined in Scripture, and conducive to morality?

133. Was the execution of the Duc D'Enghien justifiable?

134. What were the origin and nature of the Eleusinian mysteries?

135. Has any State of this Union a right of secession?

136. Is intervention by one nation in the affairs of another expedient?

137. Ought a parent, who can avoid it, ever to intrust the education of his child to persons not directly responsible to himself?

138. Does morality keep pace with the progress of civilization?

139. Is sporting justifiable?

140. Ought the United States Government to establish a national system of education?

141. Is genius innate?

142. Which has done the greater service to the cause of truth, philosophy or poetry?

143. Is there ground to believe that the atrocity of Richard III. has been greatly overstated?

144. Which was superior, Matilda, wife of William the Conqueror, or Katharine, wife of Henry VIII.?

145. Are the confessions made by the Earl of Bothwell immediately before his death, relative to Lord Darnley's death, to be regarded as true?

146. What country at the present time is under the best government?

147. Was the execution of the Earl of Essex justifiable?

148. Which is the greater discovery, that of the magnetic needle or the electric telegraph?

149. Did the writings of Junius exercise a beneficial influence upon the political condition of England?

150. Did the reign of George IV. prove beneficial to England?

151. Ought the celebration of the birthdays of great men to be en-encouraged?

152. Which was the greater man, considered as a reformer, Peter, the Great, of Russia, or Henry VIII. of England?

153. Which is the most civilized and enlightened country of the present time?

154. Were the American Indians the aborigines of this continent?

155. Is Mnemotechny beneficial?

156. Is the story of the Trojan war credible?

157. Is the cultivation of the Fine Arts always conducive to virtuous principle?

158. Have savages a full right to the soil?

159. Are political improvements better effected by rulers than by the people?

160. Is the character of a nation affected by its climate?

161. Ought representatives to be bound by the will of their constituents?

162. Is crime prevented or produced by our present system of prison discipline?

163. Which is the superior historian, Thucydides or Tacitus?

164. Ought witnesses to be held as prisoners?

165. Ought any portion of the earnings of a prisoner, during his confinement, to be allowed him upon his release?

166. Ought jurors to be paid?

167. Ought the sale of ardent spirits, for use as a beverage, to be prohibited by law?

168. Was the action of the United States government in affording protection to Martin Koszta justifiable and expedient?

169. Is it not equally the interest of the poor and the rich to prevent exorbitant taxation?

170. Who is the hero of Paradise Lost?

171. Is card-playing a safe and justifiable amusement?

172. Ought suicide to be taken as evidence of courage, or of cowardice?

173. Was the execution of Major André justifiable?

174. Which is the better guaranty of success in the world, tact or talent?

175. Has more good than evil resulted to the world from the life and religion ot Mahomet?

176. Which is the more advantageous to a country, coal mines or gold mines?

177. Has the favor shown to great statesmen in this country been such as to encourage young men of talent to qualify themselves thoroughly for high political position?

178. Has sectarianism done more to advance than to retard the interests of Christianity?

179. Which is the more useful in society, the farmer or the mechanic?

180. Are the masses governed more by fashion than by reason?

181. Is the sentiment, "*Whatever is, is right*," a just one?

182. Will the Know Nothings exert a favorable influence upon the institutions of our country?

183. Is it a wise policy to deal with our friends as though they might become our enemies?

184. Is there such a quality as disinterestedness?

185. Is the maxim, "*Our country, right or wrong*," a justifiable one?

186. Do present appearances indicate the overthrow of the British empire?

187. Ought not flagrant ingratitude to be a penal offense?

188. Ought Patent-Rights to be granted?

189. Does the present state of society in Europe portend the establishment of republican forms of government?

190. Ought parochial schools to be encouraged?

191. Does virtue always insure happiness?

192. Is the assertion, "*A little learning is a dangerous thing*," true?

193. Which do men naturally prefer, truth or error?

194. Was the last war of the United States with England justifiable?

195. Which does society most injury, the slanderer, the robber, or the murderer?

196. Did the career of Napoleon Bonaparte produce more *good* than *evil* results?

197. Is it ever advisable to act from *policy* rather than from *principle?*

198. Does *wealth* exert more influence than *knowledge?*

199. Ought *circumstantial* evidence to be admitted in criminal cases?

200. Is a Republican form of government favorable to the cultivation of literature and science?

201. Which yields the higher mental enjoyment, fact or fiction?

202. Is the English language likely ever to be universally prevalent?

203. Ought there to be a property qualification to entitle one to hold a political office?

204. Ought the right of suffrage to be dependent upon any property qualification?

205. May an oath, taken under circumstances of stress or deception, be violated without guilt?

206. Ought man to be confined to an exclusively vegetable diet?

207. Does the Bible prohibit judicial oaths?

208. Is pride commendable?

209. Ought the Missouri Compromise to have been abrogated?

210. Which is worse, a *bad* education, or *no* education?

211. Is any government as important and sacred as the principles which it is established to protect?

212. Are banks more beneficial than injurious to a community?

213. Which is preferable, genius without application, or application without genius?

214. Ought military schools to be encouraged?

215. Does not a written political constitution serve rather to hinder than to aid in securing the objects contemplated in its formation?

216. Have Byron's works an immoral tendency?

217. Did the French Revolution aid the cause of liberty in Europe?

218. Ought the private property of stockholders to be holden for the debts of a bank?

219. Would the peaceful cession of the Canadas to the United States be mutually beneficial to our own government and Great Britain?

220. Ought a judge to be influenced by the former character of a criminal?

221. Has Spain received any material benefit from her colonies?

222. Were the Olympic and other ancient games beneficial?

223. Ought public men, on retiring from office, in this country, to be pensioned?

224. Is the present general mode of celebrating the Fourth of July beneficial to the country?

225. Are different grades, or classes in society, inseparable from the present social system?

226. Would it be a wise policy for the United States to establish a large and powerful navy?

227. Should Universities be under the control of the State?

228. Is English aristocracy of birth likely to continue a political force?

229. Are rents the causes of the high price of produce?

230. Must the price of agricultural products rise with increase of wealth and population?

231. Can there be a general over-production of commodities?

232. Is there any real danger of over-population?

233. Do our institutions demand profound statesmen?

234. Can any government be kept from oppression?

235. Ought the man who kills his antagonist in a duel to be punished as a murderer?

236. Can a knowledge of human nature, in general, and of individual character in particular, be best derived from the study of history?

237. Are the United States under deeper obligations to her warriors than to her statesmen?

238. Is prosperity favorable to the morals of a nation?

239. Which afford the better opportunities for personal advancement, politics or literature?

240. Which has proved the more useful to mankind, the invention of the mariner's compass or the application of steam to navigation?

241. Which is the most powerful stimulant to exertion, emulation, patronage, or personal necessity?

242. Would a division of the Union be beneficial?

243. Is labor a blessing or a curse?

244. Ought anonymous publications to be suppressed by law?

245. Ought the surplus revenues to be distributed by Congress for the prosecution of internal improvements?

246. Were the revolutions which took place in France, between the execution of Louis XVI. and the final restoration of Louis XVIII., beneficial to that country?

247. Do the signs of the times indicate a subversion of our government?

248. Ought a military spirit to be encouraged in a country?

249. Were the principles of the Jeffersonian administration beneficial to the country?

250. Ought the rate of interest on money to be regulated by law?

251. Are national celebrations beneficial?

252. Ought there to be in this country an order of men devoted exclusively to literature?

253. Are voluntary associations for the promotion of moral principles beneficial?

254. Is a State Legislature justifiable in violating its contracts?

255. Have the administrations of our country pursued a correct policy in relation to the Indians?

256. Is man accountable for his opinions?

257. Ought a militiary chieftain to be the chief civil magistrate of a free people?

258. Ought infidels to be admitted to public office?

259. Is direct taxation preferable to indirect?

260. Ought Parliament to interfere with the revenues of the English Church?

261. Which was the more acute and profound thinker, John C. Calhoun or Daniel Webster?

262. Ought juries to be judges of the law as well as of the fact?

263. Ought clergymen to be excluded from civil offices by law?

264. Is the system of paper currency safe?

265. Ought a President of the United States to be eligible a second time to office?

266. Is difference of talent owing chiefly to nature or circumstances?

267. Are the rights of women duly regarded in the present constitution of society?

268. Is expediency the foundation of right?

269. Which has the greater influence in the foundation of national character, physical or moral causes?

270. Ought government to indemnify individuals for damages done by mobs?

271. Ought an infidel to be allowed to testify in a court of justice?

272. Ought a horse, or other beast of burden, when unable, by age or otherwise, to labor, to be killed, or turned out to die?

273. Is the maxim, "*Better that ten guilty persons should escape than that one innocent man should suffer,*" on the whole just and true?

274. Is there more of happiness than misery in human life?

275. Are tea and coffee, as beverages, injurious?

276. Ought the reading of the Bible, as a religious exercise, to be forbidden or neglected in our common schools?

277. Which is the more desirable, a state of liberty without property, or a state of property without liberty?

278. Is not the giving of military command to persons who have never seen service, a discouragement to the army?

279. Is the law of primogeniture just and expedient?

280. Is mere refinement of manners conducive to virtue?

281. Which is the more likely to procure general estimation, the reality of virtue or the appearance of it?

282. Ought foreign emigration to be encouraged?

283. Does the mind always think?

284. Is the glory of a victory, as a general thing, due more to the skill of the commander than to the bravery of the soldiers?

285. Is a lie ever justifiable?

286. Is animal magnetism altogether supernatural in its nature and operation, or is it a science founded upon natural laws?

287. Ought religious tests to be required of civil officers?

288. Ought the education of males and females to be similar in degree and kind?

289. Ought females to learn and practice the art of public speaking?

290. Ought the Bible to be employed as an ordinary reading book in schools?

291. Had the celebrated apologue, entitled "REYNARD, THE FOX," an exclusively political aim.*

292. Were the ancient oracles due to supernatural agency?

293. Is homeopathy worthy of confidence?

294. Ought eloquence to be studied as an art?

295. Is the doctrine of non-resistance sound?

296. Would the extinction of the Ottoman empire result in benefit to Europe?

297. Was the Roman conquest beneficial to Britain?

298. Were the institutions of chivalry beneficial to mankind?

299. Were the first settlers of this country justifiable in taking forcible possession of the country?

300. Which furnishes the most interesting subjects of investigation, the mineral, the animal, or the vegetable kingdom?

301. Are differences of character attributable more to physical than to moral causes?

302. Is the preservation of the balance of power in Europe a justifiable cause of war?

303. Does the present aspect of affairs in Europe give pledge or prospect of the speedy establishment of genuine liberty in that quarter of the world?

304. Is the charge of ingratitude, so often brought against Republics, founded in truth?

305. Which did the greater service to mankind, Columbus or Sir Isaac Newton?

306. Would a general European war be beneficial to the interests of this country?

* See, on this question, the "Foreign Quarterly Review," No. XXXIV., Art. III.

307. Has the restoration of Greece to political independence been on the whole beneficial?

308. Has the introduction of machinery been, on the whole, beneficial to the laboring classes?

309. Is transportation a justifiable mode of punishment?

310. Was the ostracism, practiced in ancient Athens, justifiable?

311. Which is the more pernicious character, the slanderer or the flatterer?

312. Is the system of hydropathy, or water-cure, entitled to confidence?

313. Is the attention paid to politics by all classes favorable to patriotism?

314. Is not refinement, according to the notions of the present day, unfavorable to happiness?

315. Does nature teach the doctrine or notion of a plurality of Deities?

316. Does the existence of different religious denominations tend to advance or to retard the cause of Christ?

317. Should a man ever praise his own work?

318. Is the doctrine of innate ideas founded in truth?

319. Should the truth always be spoken?

320. Which gives the better insight into human nature, reading or observation?

321. Which afford the better field for the display of originality, the Fine or the Useful Arts?

322. Which is the more interesting and instructive, Grecian or Roman history?

323. Which is the more valuable, physical or moral courage?

324 Ought secret societies to be tolerated?

325. Would any further extension of the Union be politic?

326. Has Christianity been a temporal as well as a spiritual blessing to the world?

327. Is the temporal essential to the spiritual jurisdiction of the Pope?

328. Ought a man to marry his deceased wife's sister?

329. Can the immortality of the soul be proved from the light of nature?

330. Ought a representative always to be an inhabitant of the town or district represented?

331. Which is preferable, city or country life?

332. Is resistance to the constituted authorities in the State ever justifiable?

333. Ought emulation in schools to be encouraged?

334. Which is the more conducive to the cultivation of literature, a monarchical or a republican form of government?

335. Has a man a right to expatriate himself?

336. Is teaching a profession in the same sense, that law, medicine and theology are professions?

337. Is Madison more deserving our estimation than Hamilton?

338. Is dueling ever justifiable?

339. Ought theatres to be abolished?

340. Which is preferable, anarchy or despotism?

341. Is the American Colonization Society worthy of national support?

342. Can the North Pole be reached by navigation?

343. Would the acquisition of Cuba by the United States be beneficial to the latter?

344. Is it possible to determine the true nature and origin of meteors?

345. Is the natural state of man, as asserted by Hobbes, a state of war?

346. Was Cicero greater as an orator than as a philosopher?

347. Is the habitual use of tobacco for chewing and smoking injurious to health?

348. Is the doctrine of endless punishment taught in the Bible?

349. Has Junius ever been identified?

350. Have we anything to fear from the spread of Popery?

351. Was the Atlantis of the ancients identical with the continent of America?

352. Is corporal punishment necessary in the schools?

353. Should a boy be taught those things only which he is likely to need in practical life when a man?

354. Ought not Sunday-schools, in which the Bible is taught without reference to sectarian differences, to be supported by the public funds?

355. Are the ideas of the mind separate from the mind itself?

356. Is it wise in a parent to labor to amass money in order to leave a rich inheritance to his children?

357. Is there sufficient ground for the belief, that the career of Joan of Arc was due to supernatural agency?

358. Is the character of Aaron Burr justly estimated?

359. Can utility be considered as a safe moral guide?

360. Do modern biographies generally give a fair insight into human character?

361. Was Warren Hastings' conduct in India justifiable?

362. Are short terms of political office desirable?

363. Which is the most prolific source of crime, poverty, wealth, or ignorance?

364. Which is superior, as an intellectual gymnastic, a classical or a mathematical education?

365. Is capital punishment justifiable?

366. Should the main end of punishment be the reformation of the criminal or the prevention of crime?

367. Which furnishes the better safeguard against crime, the jail or the school?

368. Which is the better government, a limited monarchy or a republic?

369. Is true eloquence the gift of nature or of art?

370. Which is the more extensively useful, *fire* or *water?*

371. Is it ever right to marry for money?

372. Ought our country to establish and endow a national university?

373. Is it expedient to wear mourning apparel?

374. Which is the stronger inducement to the study of history, the *love of truth*, or mere *curiosity?*

375. Has the study of mythology an immoral tendency?

376. Which did the greater mischief, Mahomet or Constantine?

377. Is there any necessary connection between *genius* and *eccentricity?*

378. Have not the defenses of Christianity been rather strengthened than weakened by the assaults of infidelity?

379. Ought a man to be influenced in respect to the fashion of his apparel by a regard to the opinions or practice of others?

380. Would the public morals be injured by the non-observance of the Christian Sabbath?

381. Ought truth ever to be withheld on the ground, that the world is not prepared to receive it?

382. Is it expedient to make authorship a business or profession?

383. Is the judgment of conscience always correct?

384. Which is the more disadvantageous, credulity or skepticism?

385. Which gives the more clear and forcible ideas of scenes and actions, the poet or the painter?

386. Which is the more selfish person, the miser or the profligate?

387. Ought one ever to advocate or defend what he believes to be false?

388. Ought persons of foreign birth to be allowed the right of suffrage?

389. Ought government officers to be confined exclusively to native citizens?

390. Have Sir Walter Scott's writings been beneficial in their influence?

391. Is the system of American slavery more odious and unjust than Russian serfdom?

392. Which offers the better field for the cultivation of eloquence, the bar or the pulpit?

393. Is the law an honorable profession?

394. Ought public school-money to be appropriated exclusively to common schools?

395. Does proselytism favor the cause of truth?

396. Should military achievements influence the election of President of the United States of America?

397. Would the suppression of civil and religious liberty in Europe have a tendency to destroy our own?

398. Is the maxim, "*Every man is the architect of his own fortune,*" true?

399. Is war ever justifiable?

400. Should letters of marque and reprisal be granted?

401. Is the advancement of civil liberty indebted more to intellectual culture than to physical suffering?

402. Is nature alone sufficient to teach man his duty to God?

403. Which has caused more evil, ambition or intemperance?

404. Does not the persecution of any principle or party tend more to its advancement than the works of its own supporters?

405. Are any of the so-called spiritual manifestations of the present day properly referable to the agency of departed spirits?

406. Is the supply of coal from the mines likely always to be equal to the wants of the world?

407. Ought the aim of education to be the harmonious development of all its powers, or the special training of individual faculties?

408. Has popular superstition a favorable influence on the literature of a nation?

409. In the present European struggle has the true spirit of human freedom been manifested?

410. Was the political career of Oliver Cromwell beneficial to Great Britain?

411. Is our country in more danger from external factions than from internal foes?

412. Was the claim of Texas upon New Mexico invalid?

413. Is the inebriate accountable to God for the crimes he commits while intoxicated?

414. Which is the more effective in government, force or persuasion?

415. Have false systems of religion caused more misery than false systems of government?

416. Would an intuitive knowledge of all we are capable of comprehending, contribute to increase our happiness beyond that of our present state?

417. Would an equalization of property conduce to the happiness of society?

418. Is not the rank held by women in a community the best test of the morals of that community?

419. Is the Union likely to be perpetual?

420. Will republicanism eventually supersede all other forms of government?

421. Has the enthronement of Napoleon III. benefited France?

422. Ought the French and English to have joined the Turks against Russia?

423. Have we reason to conclude that other planets than our own are inhabited?

424. Are the Indians generally capable of being civilized?

425. Will African slavery be perpetual in the United States?

426. Ought Free-Masonry to be responsible for the murder of Morgan?

427. Is a Reciprocity Treaty between the United States and Canada desirable?

428. Is the popularity of a literary production a sure test of its merit?

429. Is human life capable of any essential prolongation by human means?

430. Is the literature of a nation affected by its form of government?

431. Is the system of internal improvements politic?

432. Is the reasoning indicated in the famous aphorism of Descartes, "*Cogito, ergo sum,*" (I *think*, therefore I *exist*,) conclusive?

433. Is there evidence sufficient, apart from the Bible, to prove the existence, at some former period, of a universal deluge?

434. Was the execution of Charles I. justifiable?

435. Should the United States undertake to control the political movements of this continent?

436. Is modern equal to ancient patriotism?

437. Which is preferable, moral or physical courage?

438. Are debating societies beneficial?

439. Ought the Lancasterian system of teaching to be encouraged?

440. Ought the President of the United States to be invested with the veto power?

441. Are the educated classes more virtuous, on the whole, than the ignorant?

442. Are there any signs of decay in poetry and art?

443. Does the eighteenth century deserve the eulogium pronounced upon it by Guizot?

444. Is there any great advantage in indirect elections?

445. Is language a human invention?

446. Ought the quantity of land held by one person to be limited?

447. Is the literary inferiority of the American nation owing to its infancy?

448. Ought unanimity to be required that the verdict of a jury may have force?

449. Could England maintain her present superiority without an aristocratic class?

450. Ought civilization to be propagated by force?

451. Is the United States in danger from an aristocratic class?

452. Can republican forms of government exist without public virtue?

453. Ought Congress to prohibit carrying and distributing the mail on Sunday?

454. Was the American revolution justifiable on moral grounds?

455. Are the crimes among barbarians more numerous or more heinous, as a general thing, than those among civilized men?

456. Is a lawyer justifiable in defending a person whom he knows to be guilty?

457. Was Brutus justifiable in taking part with the conspirators against Cæsar?

458. Ought a republican government to tolerate all religious denominations?

459. Were O'Connel and those indicted with him justly convicted?

460. Ought a student in college to direct his studies with reference to a particular profession?

461. Was Swedenborg mistaken in the belief, that he was admitted into intercourse with the invisible world?

462. Should monuments be erected to the illustrious dead?

463. Is liberty one of man's rights?

464. Have pride and ambition caused more evil than ignorance and superstition?

465. Are American churches the bulwark of liberty?

466. Does spirituous liquor cause more evil than money?

467. Is man governed more by moral than by civil laws?

468. Would a universal language be desirable?

469. Has light reading or social intercourse the better effect in preparing one for usefulness?

470. Which is the more prolific source of enjoyment, memory or imagination?

471. Which have conferred the higher benefit on their country, the poets or prose writers of England?

472. Is the doctrine of ministerial parity fairly deducible from the Bible?

473. Are the poetical parts of the Bible, considered merely as literary productions, inferior to the poems of Homer or Milton?

474. Is poverty oftener the result of misfortune than of mismanagement?

475. Which exerts the greater influence on the happiness of mankind, the male or the female mind?

476. Have the lost tribes of Israel ever been discovered?

477. Ought mixed schools* to be encouraged?

478. Has not fashion a tendency to pervert the judgment?

479. Should parties be compelled to give evidence in civil cases?

480. Ought the robbery of the grave to be punished as felony?

481. Was the reign of Henry VIII. advantageous to the liberties of England?

482. Was the death of Cæsar beneficial to Rome?

483. Ought Coriolanus to have made war against his country?

484. Was the feudal system beneficial?

485. Is alcohol, considered in respect to all its various uses, more injurious than beneficial to mankind?

486. Was the Roman conquest beneficial to Britain?

487. Was the monastic system beneficial to the interests of science?

488. Were the institutions of chivalry beneficial to mankind?

489. Would Regulus have been justified in not returning to Carthage?

490. Does civilization tend to abolish military ambition?

* That is, schools wherein males and females are taught together in the same classes.

491. Are the present facilities of intercourse between Europe and the United States favorable to the latter?

492. Which is the greater deprivation, loss of sight or loss of hearing?

493. Is the designation, "*Irritabile genus*,"* so often applied to authors, just.

494. Is there any authoritative standard of taste?

495. Do modern discoveries in geological science serve to confirm or weaken our faith in the Mosaic account of the creation?

496. Was the execution of Mary Queen of Scots justifiable?

497. Can there be a virtuous ambition?

498. Ought children be compelled to attend school, at certain hours, by force of law?

499. Ought street beggary to be tolerated?

500. Which is the more useful member of the community, the lawyer or the clergyman?

501. Which is the most serviceable to mankind, the farmer, the mechanic, or the merchant?

502. Ought a teacher of youth to be himself a parent?

503. Are brutes endowed with reason?

504. Is the spendthrift more injurious to society than the miser?

505. Has the invention of gunpowder proved more useful than hurtful to mankind?

506. Which is the meaner character, the liar or the hypocrite?

507. Which was the greatest general, Alexander, Hannibal, or Napoleon?

508. Ought the colonization of the African race to be encouraged?

509. Ought the election of President and Vice-President to be taken entirely from the Senate and House?

510. Ought the national government to make appropriations for internal improvements?

511. Are the moderns superior to the ancients in rhetorical science?

512. Would the peaceable accession of the Canadas be beneficial to the United States?

513. Had the allied powers a right to place a king over Greece?

514. Which is the more serviceable to his country, the statesman or the warrior?

515. Does morality advance equally with civilization?

516. Is universal peace probable?

517. Which was the greater orator, Demosthenes or Cicero?

* An irascible race.

518. Is military glory a just object of ambition?

519. Which was the more powerful agency in producing the French revolution, the tyranny of the government or the excesses of the priests and nobles?

520. Are not popular superstitions favorable to the growth of poetry?

521. Is there sufficient ground for a belief in the alleged deterioration of animals and vegetables in America?

522. Are not the public, in this country, generally deprived of the official services of our best men, by the reckless abuse of the press during election times?

523. Ought the Catholics to have a separate school fund?

524. Was Cromwell a patriot?

525. Was Napoleon's banishment to St. Helena justifiable?

526. Ought a representative to be bound by the will of his constituents?

527. Should government prohibit private mails?

528. Is it probable a republican government will be the prevailing one in the world?

529. Were circumstances in past ages as favorable to the growth of literature as they are at present?

530. Should the present popularity of a literary work be taken as an index of its real merits?

531. Ought a college or university to be located in the city or in the country?

532. Ought a man to propose himself for a public office and advocate his own claims to preferment?

533. Is Puseyism compatible with Protestantism?

534. Is man a free moral agent?

535. Has the love of money more influence upon mankind than education?

536. Should the laws of justice ever be turned aside to favor the cause of humanity?

537. Was the late United-States Japan expedition a just one?

538. Does not a multiplicity of books rather clog than deepen the channels of learning?

539. Is the character of Jefferson worthy of admiration?

540. Was the execution of Lady Jane Grey justifiable?

541. Was it not the purpose of Shakspeare to delineate, in the conduct of Desdemona, a character really indelicate and even unnatural, though apparently noble, refined, and every way commendable?

542. Was there a greater field for eloquence in ancient than in modern times?

543. Was the bankrupt law justifiable?

544. Are our liberties more endangered by aristocracy than democracy?

545. Were the crusades beneficial?

546. Is party spirit beneficial to a country?

547. Is a fugitive slave justified in taking the property of others to aid his escape?

548. Is offensive war justifiable in any case?

549. Has the discovery of the New World benefited mankind?

550. Are newspapers beneficial to the community at large?

551. Does the turpitude of a crime consist wholly in the intention?

552. Are populous cities beneficial to a country?

553. Is there reason to believe that the sages and philosophers of antiquity secretly discredited the popular religious systems of their day?

554. Is Pope's "Essay on Man" justly chargeable with an infidel tendency?

555. Ought universal suffrage to be allowed?

556. Ought ambition to be used as a motive for educating youth?

557. Was the conquest of Granada by Ferdinand and Isabella justifiable?

558. Is Hogarth's theory, respecting the fundamental source, or principle of beauty, correct?

559. Was Kossuth justifiable in resigning his post as governor of Hungary into the hands of Görgy, and in fleeing his country?

560. Is the practice of reciting the speeches of others, as an exercise in elocution, on the whole, beneficial?

561. Is it really a measure of prudence to issue what are termed "*expurgated editions of the classics?*"

562. Does universal suffrage lead men to value electoral rights?

563. Which is the more useful to society, intellectual or physical labor?

564. Can we profit more by the excellences than by the defects of others?

565. Is the character of Archbishop Laud, generally, justly estimated?

566. Which is the more effective external means of securing favor, dress or address?

567. Which is the more destructive element, fire or water?

568. Can any process of reasoning take place in the mind, without the aid of language, orally or mentally?

569. Had the ancients more virtue than the moderns?

570. Is prejudice a sin?

571. Is there more to approve than condemn in the character of Oliver Cromwell?

572. Which has been the more serviceable to mankind, the printing-press or the steam-engine?

573. Is the maxim, "*Where there's a will, there's a way,*" always true?

574. Would it be of advantage to fix the rate of wages by law?

575. Is there an absolute standard of honor, as of right?

576. Is the maxim, that "*Men should surrender some of their rights,*" safe and just?

577. Do democratic institutions promote a desirable form of manners and character?

578. Are there more worlds than ono?

579. Are early marriages conducive to the well-being of society?

580. Is it a wise policy for Americans to send their children into foreign countries to be educated?

581. Ought the right of church property to be vested exclusively in Bishops or any other ecclesiastical dignitaries?

582. Which of the lower animals is the most useful to mankind?

SECTION XIV.

FORMS OF A CONSTITUTION AND BY-LAWS SUITABLE FOR A LITERARY OR DEBATING SOCIETY.

IT being one of the first duties, upon the formation of a Literary or Debating Society, to provide a system of rules and regulations, whereby the objects of the society may be more certainly secured, it is customary, for that purpose, to appoint a committee to draft a suitable constitution, as also such by-laws as may seem expedient.

In so doing, it is convenient and useful to have at hand forms which have already been submitted to the test of experience; for these serve as guides in ascertaining what has elsewhere, under the like circumstances, been found necessary or desirable.

And, although every essential aid, perhaps, in cases of this kind, might be found in that part of the present work* which treats of the Rules of Order in Deliberative Assemblies, still, that nothing, in this regard, may be wanting, we present, in this Section, literal copies of the constitutions and by-laws of two societies now in successful operation. Of course, they are not given as models to be implicitly followed, but as *forms to be altered, modified, and adapted to circumstances.* It is wisdom to avail ourselves of the experience of others.

* Sections IV. and V.

CONSTITUTION AND BY-LAWS*

OF THE

YOUNG MEN'S

AMERICAN SOCIAL AND DEBATING CLUB

OF THE CITY OF NEW YORK

PREAMBLE.

WHEREAS it is necessary, in order to fit ourselves for the varied duties of life, to cultivate a correct mode of speaking, and to qualify ourselves, by practice, to express our opinions in public, in a correct manner; and, whereas the extension of our information upon all subjects calculated to improve the mind, is highly commendable, and, as experience has abundantly proved that these ends can in no other way be so speedily accomplished as by forming a Club for such a purpose; therefore, we, the undersigned, have organized a Club, and have adopted for our government the following Constitution, By-Laws, Rules and Regutions.

* We give, as before said, *literal copies* of these constitutions and by-laws: not feeling at liberty to alter either their language or their provisions, however much we might wish them, in some particulars, to be otherwise.

CONSTITUTION.

ARTICLE I.

NAME.

This Club shall be known as the YOUNG MEN'S AMERICAN SOCIAL and DEBATING CLUB of the City of New-York.

ARTICLE II.

OBJECTS.

The objects of this Club shall be the improvement of all connected with it, in debating, social advancement, and general literature. All questions bordering on immorality, or sectarian, shall be excluded.

ARTICLE III.

MEMBERSHIP.

Clause 1.—None other than Americans, over the age of fifteen, and under the age of twenty-five, are eligible for membership.

Clause 2.—Persons of any age may be elected Honorary Members of this Club, by a unanimous ballot; but they shall not be entitled to hold office, nor to vote.

ARTICLE IV.

OFFICERS.

The officers of this Club shall consist of a President, Vice-President, Secretary and Treasurer, all of whom shall be voted for, separately, by ballot.

ARTICLE V.

DUTIES OF PRESIDENT.

It shall be the duty of the President to preside at all meetings of the Club, and enforce a rigid observance of the Constitution, By-Laws, Rules and Regulations of the Club; appoint all Committees, unless otherwise ordered: see that the officers perform their respective duties; inspect and announce the result of all ballotings, or other votes; in all cases of balloting he shall be permitted to vote; in other cases he shall not vote, except in case of a tie, when he shall give the casting vote; in balloting, if there should be a tie twice in succession, he shall then give the casting vote except in case of election of officers; he shall neither make nor second any motion, neither shall he take part in any debate while in the chair; to draw upon the Treasurer for all sums that may have been voted for; and to have a general superintendence of the business of the Club.

ARTICLE VI.

DUTIES OF VICE-PRESIDENT.

It shall be the duty of the Vice-President to preside in the absence of the President, and perform the duties of that officer.

ARTICLE VII.

DUTIES OF SECRETARY.

It shall be the duty of the Secretary to keep the minutes of the Club, notify candidates of their election, register the names of the members, issue all notices required, and perform such other duties pertaining to his office as may be required of him by the Club. At the first meeting in every month, he shall present a written report of the state of the Club; and its doings during the past month.

ARTICLE VIII.

DUTIES OF TREASURER.

It shall be the duty of the Treasurer to take care of all moneys and property belonging to the Club, and keep a written account of all moneys received or expended; and, at the first meeting in every month, present a written report of the financial condition of the Club.

ARTICLE IX.

ELECTION OF OFFICERS.

Clause 1.—All the officers of this Club shall be elected by ballot to serve a term of four months.

Clause 2.—They shall be elected at the first regular meeting in January, May and September, and installed on the first regular meeting succeeding their election.

Clause 3.—No person can be elected to an office, until he has been a member of this Club one month.

Clause 4.—A majority of all legal votes cast shall be necessary to a choice.

ARTICLE X.

REMOVALS FROM OFFICE.

Clause 1.—Should any officer or member of a committee neglect or be found incompetent to discharge the duties of his office, he may be removed by a vote of three fourths of the members present.

Clause 2. All places of absentees in committees may be filled by said committees.

ARTICLE XI.

AMENDMENTS.

No addition, alteration or amendment can be made to this Constitution—neither can any part of it be repealed, without a two-third vote of the Club, and one month's previous notice.

BY-LAWS.

ARTICLE I.

MEETINGS.

SEC. 1.—This Club shall assemble on the first and third Wednesdays of each month, unless otherwise ordered, for the promotion of its objects, and the transaction of its business.

SEC. 2.—This club shall meet annually on the 22d of February, to celebrate the birth-day of the Father of our Country, at such place as the Club may direct.

SEC. 3.—Special meetings may be called by the President, at the written request of five members.

SEC. 4.—The hour of meeting from the first Wednesday in April to the first Wednesday in September, shall be at eight o'clock P. M., and from the first Wednesday in September to the first Wednesday in April, at 7½ o'clock P. M.

ARTICLE II.

QUORUM.

At any meeting of the Club, two thirds of the members shall constitute a quorum.

ARTICLE III.

MEMBERSHIP.

SEC. 1.—Members intending to propose a candidate for membership, shall submit his birthplace, name, age, residence and occupation to the Club. A committee shall then be appointed by the chair, (not consisting of the person who proposed him,) said committee to visit the candidate personally, with the Constitution and By-Laws, and to report to the Club.

SEC. 2.—After the report has been disposed of, the Club shall proceed to ballot for the candidate, and should two thirds of the ballot be for admission, he may be initiated (if present) at the same meeting. But should he not present himself for initiation within six weeks, (unless a sufficient reason be given,) his election shall become void.

SEC. 3.—No candidate rejected shall be proposed again for membership within three months.

SEC. 4.—Every candidate, upon being initiated, shall sign the Constitution and By-Laws of the Club, and thereby agree to support the same, and pay all legal demands against him as long as he remains a member.

ARTICLE IV.

INITIATION FEE.

All persons initiated into this Club, shall pay the sum of fifty cents upon being initiated. No person shall be entitled to the privileges of a member, until said initiation fee is paid.

ARTICLE V.

DUES.

Every member shall pay the sum of twenty-five cents monthly, in advance, into the treasury.

ARTICLE VI.

FINES.

The Chair shall have the power to impose the following fines:

SEC. 1.—Any member who shall, at the meetings, make use of any improper language, or refuse to obey the commands of the President when called to order, or be guilty of any disorderly conduct, shall be fined for each offense *ten cents.*

SEC. 2.—If any member absent himself from the meetings two evenings in succession, unless a satisfactory excuse be given, he shall be fined *ten cents.*

SEC. 3.—Any member who shall leave the Club before closing, without permission from the President, shall be fined *ten cents.*

SEC. 4.—If a member appointed to serve on a committee neglects to attend to its duties, he shall, unless he presents a satisfactory excuse, be fined *ten cents.*

SEC. 5.—Should the Secretary, Treasurer, or any officer, neglect to have at the meetings such books and papers belonging to the Club as may be necessary to use; or neglect to perform his duties, as laid down in the Constitution and By-Laws, he shall, unless a satisfactory excuse is given, be fined for each offense *ten cents.*

SEC. 6.—Should a committee be hindered in the performance of its duty through the negligence of any officer, said officer shall be fined *ten cents.*

SEC. 7.—If a member neglect to pay his fines or assessments within two weeks after being imposed, he shall be fined *ten cents;* and for each additional week *five cents.*

SEC. 8.—Should any member refuse to conform to the Rules of Debate, &c., he shall suffer such penalties as are there laid down.

SEC. 9.—For such acts of negligence, and neglect of duty, as are not noticed in the above sections, the Chair, with the consent of the Club, may impose a fine not exceeding *twenty-five cents.*

ARTICLE VII.

APPEALS.

Any member shall have the right, when fined, to appeal from the decision of the Chair to the meeting; and, unless the Club sustain the position of the Chair, said fine shall be remitted.

ARTICLE VIII.

The Club may fine the President, while presiding, for any neglect of duty, *ten cents.*

ARTICLE IX.

ARREARAGES.

SEC. 1.—No member in arrears for dues more than four weeks, or fines to the amount of fifty cents, shall be privileged to vote or speak on any question, until said arrearages are paid.

SEC. 2.—Every member who shall refuse or neglect to pay his dues for the space of two weeks, shall be notified thereof by the Secretary, if practicable, and if, after four weeks thereafter, his account remains unsettled, he shall stand suspended; and shall not be reinstated, until all dues and arrearages against him shall be paid.

SEC. 3.—Any member who shall be in arrears to the Club to the amount of two dollars, shall be suspended; and should his account remain unsettled four weeks thereafter, he shall be expelled.

ARTICLE X.

TAX.

If the funds of this Club should, at any time, be exhausted, or inadequate to meet its demands, there shall be an equal tax upon each member to make up the deficiency.

ARTICLE XI.

SUSPENSION AND EXPULSION.

SEC. 1.—Any member who shall refuse to conform to the Constitution, By-Laws, Rules and Regulations of this Club, or be guilty of repeated disorderly conduct, shall be subject to suspension or expulsion.

SEC. 2.—When the motion for the expulsion of a member shall have been made, it shall be announced at two regular meetings previous to action being taken, when the accused shall be permitted to show reasons why he should not be expelled. If, however, two thirds of the members present vote in favor of the motion it shall be carried, and under no circumstances can it be reconsidered.

SEC. 3.—Members expelled cannot be proposed again for membership, within one year.

SEC. 4.—Any member who resigns from this Club, can not become a member again, until all dues, from the time he left the Club, be paid up in full.

ARTICLE XII.

AMENDMENTS.

No addition, alteration, or amendment, can be made to these By-Laws; neither can any part of them be repealed, without a two-third vote of the Club, and one month's previous notice.

RULES OF ORDER.

RULE 1.—No question shall be stated, unless moved by two members, nor be open for consideration, until stated by the Chair. When a question is before the Club, no motion shall be received, except to lay on the table, the previous question, to postpone, to refer, or to amend, and they shall have precedence in the order, in which they are arranged.

RULE 2.—When a member intends to speak on a question, he shall rise in his place, and respectfully address his remarks to the President, confine himself to the question, and avoid personality. Should more than one member rise to speak, at the same time, the President shall determine who is entitled to the floor.

RULE 3.—Every member shall have the privilege of speaking twice on any question under consideration, but not oftener, unless by consent of the President; and no member shall speak more than once, until any member wishing to speak shall have spoken.

RULE 4.—The President, while presiding, shall state every question coming before the Club, and immediately before putting it to vote, shall ask: "Are you ready for the question?" Should no member rise to speak, he shall rise to take the question; and after he has risen, no member shall speak upon it, unless by permission of the President.

RULE 5.—The affirmative and negative of the question having been both put and answered, the President declares whether the affirmative or negative have it, being himself satisfied which is the greater; but, if he be not, or if before any member enters or leaves the Club, a member shall rise and declare himself dissatisfied with the President's decision, then the President shall divide the Club.

Rule 6.—Any three members calling for the yeas and nays, they shall be ordered by the President, and recorded on the minutes. Each qualified member present shall, when called upon for his vote, declare openly and without debate, his assent or dissent to the question, unless he be excused by the Club.

Rule 7.—All questions, unless otherwise fixed by law, shall be determined by a majority of votes.

Rule 8.—After any question, except one of indefinite postponement, has been decided, any member may move a reconsideration thereof, if done in two weeks after the decision. A motion for a reconsideration the second time, of the same question, shall not be in order at any time.

Rule 9.—Any two members may call for a division of a question, when the same will admit of it.

Rule 10.—The President, or any member, may call a member to order, while speaking, when the debate must be suspended, and the member takes his seat until the question of order is decided.

Rule 11.—The President shall preserve order and decorum; may speak to points of order in preference to other members; and shall decide all questions of order, subject to an appeal to the Club by any member; on which appeal no person shall speak but the President, and the member called to order.

Rule 12.—No motion or proposition on a subject

different from that under consideration, shall be admitted under color of an amendment.

Rule 13.—Every motion shall be reduced to writing, should the President, Secretary, or any two members desire it.

Rule 14.—All Resolutions, and Reports of Committees, shall be presented in writing, and signed by the members offering the same.

Rule 15.—A majority of a Committee constitutes a quorum for the transaction of business.

Rule 16.—An amendment to an amendment is in order, but not to amend an amendment to an amendment of a main question.

Rule 17.—The previous question shall be put in this form, if seconded by a majority of the members present: "Shall the main question now be put?" If decided in the affirmative, the main question is to be put immediately, and all further debate or amendment must be suspended.

Rule 18.—No subject laid on the table shall be taken up again on the same evening.

Rule 19.—Members not voting shall be considered as voting in the affirmative, unless excused by the Club.

Rule 20.—Any member offering a protest against any of the proceedings of this Club, may have the same, if in respectful language, entered in full upon the minutes.

Rule 21.—No alteration can be made in these rules of order without a two-third vote of the Club, and one month's notice, neither can they be suspended but by a like vote, and for the evening only.

RULES OF DEBATE.

Rule 1.—The following shall be the exercises for the promotion of the objects of the Club. On the first meeting in every month, the Club may choose one member who shall deliver a lecture, essay, or recitation.

Rule 2.—On the evening for debating, the President shall first state the subject, and the sides shall then speak alternately, if desiring; the leader of the affirmative always opening the debate, and the leader of the negative always answering. The leader of the negative only shall close the debate.

Rule 3.—In any debate, no person shall speak more than twice, without permission from the President, nor more than once, until every member wishing to speak shall have spoken. No member shall occupy the floor more than ten minutes.

Rule 4.—The presiding officer shall decide all debates according to the merits of the arguments used by either side.

Rule 5.—These rules may be altered or amended by a two-third vote of the Club; written notice of the intended alteration or amendment having been given one month previous.

ORDER OF BUSINESS.

1. Call to order.
2. Calling of the roll.

3. Reading minutes of previous meeting.
4. Propositions for membership.
5. Reports of special committees.
6. Balloting for candidates.
7. Reports of standing committees.
8. Secretary's report.
9. Treasurer's report.
10. Readings for the evening.
11. Recitations for the evening.
12. Candidates initiated.
13. Unfinished business.
14. Debate.
15. New business.
16. Adjournment.

OF FRATERNAL COURTESY.

It is particularly enjoined that the members of this Club treat each other with due delicacy and respect, and that all discussions be conducted with candor, spirit, moderation and open generosity, and that all personal allusions and sarcastic language, by which a brother's feelings may be hurt, be done away with and carefully avoided, that, in concord and good fellowship, we may cherish and preserve the *prominent* features of our Club,

FRIENDSHIP, LOVE AND TRUTH.

CONSTITUTION,

By-Laws, and Rules of Order

OF THE

ADDISONIAN SOCIETY,

OF THE CITY OF NEW YORK.

Preamble.

WE, the undersigned, do declare ourselves an Association for mutual improvement in Elocution, Composition and Debate, and for enlarging our fund of general intelligence: in the pursuit of which objects we desire to exhibit a due consideration for the opinions and feelings of others, to maintain a perfect command of temper in all our intercourse, to seek for truth in all our exercises—and have adopted for our government the following *Constitution, By-Laws, and Rules of Order.*

CONSTITUTION.

ARTICLE I.—NAME.

This Association shall be known by the name of the "ADDISONIAN SOCIETY."

ARTICLE II.—OFFICERS.

The Officers of the Association shall consist of a President, a Vice President, Recording Secretary, Corresponding Secretary, and Treasurer, who shall constitute a Board of Directors; also two Tellers and an Editor.

ARTICLE III.—OFFICERS' DUTIES.

Sec. 1.—It shall be the duty of the President to preside at all meetings of the Society, to enforce a due observance of the Constitution, By-Laws, and Rules of Order; to decide all questions of order, offer for consideration all motions regularly made, apportion duties two weeks in advance, call all special meetings, appoint all committees not otherwise provided for, and perform such other duties as his office may require. He shall make no motion or amendment, nor vote on any question or motion, unless the Society be equally divided, when he shall give the casting vote.

Sec. 2.—In the absence of the President, the Vice President shall perform the duties of that officer, and shall be Chairman of the Board of Directors.

Sec. 3.—The Recording Secretary shall keep in a book, provided for the purpose, a record of the proceedings of the Society; also a record of the name and residence of each member, showing, when he was admitted, and when he died, resigned, or was expelled; keep a record of the subjects debated, the disputants and the decisions of the Society in a separate book, and shall have charge of all books, documents and papers belonging to the Society.

Sec. 4. The Corresponding Secretary shall notify absent members of their duties for the two succeeding meetings, also each person elected a member, of such election, and shall write all communications.

Sec. 5. The Treasurer shall receive all moneys belonging to the Society; keep an account of all dues and fines, and of all receipts and expenditures; notify each member monthly of his dues and fines, and collect the same; and shall call the Roll at the opening and close of each meeting. He shall report the state of the Treasury whenever required by a resolution of the Society, and shall make no payments without a written order from the President, and countersigned by the Recording Secretary.

Sec. 6. The Editor shall copy, in a book provided for the purpose, all communications received by him, excluding such as may contain personal or improper remarks, and shall read the same at every alternate meeting of the Society. He shall maintain secresy concerning the authorship of all communications, and insert them without addition or alteration. Such periodical shall be called the "Addisonian Review."

Sec. 7. The Tellers shall canvass the votes cast at all elections; shall immediately make known the result of same, and render a true written report at the meeting following such election.

Sec. 8. The Board of Directors shall be a Standing Committee to manage the affairs of the Society, holding meetings at least once a month. They shall decide upon all questions of debate offered in the Society, and shall examine and inquire into the standing of all persons proposed for membership, and at the next regular meeting, report the result to the Society, who shall determine upon their admission.

Sec. 9. The Board of Directors and Treasurer shall present to, and read before the Society, reports at the expiration of their terms of office.

Article IV.—Election of Officers.

Sec. 1. All Elections for Officers shall be held at the last regular meetings in June and January. The term of each shall commence at the meeting following his election. In case of a vacancy occurring in any office, the Society shall go into an immediate election to fill the same, and the officer elect shall take his seat immediately after such election.

Sec. 2. All elections for officers shall be made by ballot, and shall be determined by two thirds of the votes cast.

Article V.—Membership.

Sec. 1. Any member may propose a person for membership at a regular meeting, by giving his name, residence and occupation, and after being reported upon by the Board of Directors, the Society shall determine his admission by a three-fourth vote of the members present.

Sec. 2. Any person may be elected an Honorary Member of the Society, by a unanimous vote at a regular meeting. He shall be entitled to all the privileges of a member, except holding office or voting upon any question or motion, and shall not be fined for absence, nor called upon for the initiation fee or dues.

Article VI.—Amendments to Constitution, &c.

Every proposed alteration, amendment or addition to this Constitution, By-Laws and Rules of Order hereunto annexed, must be handed to the President in writing, who shall publish the same to the Society, and at the next regular meeting, it shall be adopted by a two-third vote of the members present.

Article VII.—Order of Business.

A motion to change the Order of Business, or to postpone the performance of the regular duties, shall require, for its adoption, a vote of two thirds of the members present.

Article VIII.—Suspension of By-Laws.

A By-Law or Rule of Order may be suspended in case of an emergency, by a two-third vote of the members present, but only for a single evening.

BY-LAWS.

Article I.—Meetings.

Sec. 1. This Society shall hold its meetings, unless otherwise ordered, on Saturday evening of each week; the hour of meeting during the months of October, November, December and January, shall be at 7½ P. M., and at 8 o'clock during the rest of the year; the meetings to stand adjourned at 10½.

Sec. 2. Six members shall be necessary to constitute a quorum.

Sec. 3. At the request of six members the President shall call a special meeting of the Society. In case of absence from any special meeting, a member shall be fined in accordance with Article 5th, Section 1st, of these By-Laws.

Article II.—Inauguration of Officers.

At the inauguration of each Officer, he shall be required to make the following affirmation:

"I do hereby solemnly promise, that I will faithfully discharge the duties of my office to the best of my knowledge and ability."

Article III.—Initiation of Members.

The following affirmation shall be required of each person becoming a member:

"I do hereby solemnly promise, that I will observe and strictly obey all the laws, rules and regulations set down in the Constitution of this Society, and do further declare, that I entertain no ill-will toward any member."

Article IV.—Debates, Essays, Recitations, &c.

Sec. 1. The two Orders of Business hereunto prefixed, shall occupy alternate meetings of the Society. On the Debating evening, there shall be a general debate, which shall be opened on either side, by a member previously appointed. On the Miscellaneous evening, half of the members shall alternately perform duties, either in Essay or Recitation, as the President may have previously designated.

Sec. 2. The following questions, or such part as time will permit, shall be asked at every Miscellaneous meeting of the Society, commencing where they were left off at the previous meeting:

1st. Have you lately met with any thing calculated to interest or improve the Society, either in History, Travels, Sciences, the Arts, or other branches of useful knowledge?

2d. Do you know of any amusing story proper to relate in conversation?

3d. Have you any questions for debate to submit for the consideration of this Board?

Sec. 3. The leaders in debate shall be allowed to speak fifteen minutes each time; all others shall be limited to ten minutes.

Sec. 4. All communications intended for insertion in the "Addisonian Review," must be original, and written by members of the Society, and handed to the Editor at least three days before publication.

Article V.—Dues, Fines, &c.

Sec. 1. The Fines shall be as follows, viz.: for late attendance, non-performance of duty, disorderly conduct, and for calling to order without substantiating the point, each, five cents; for absence, (except of leaders on debate, which shall be fifteen cents,) ten cents; and for leaving the room without permission of the President, twenty-five cents.

Sec. 2. Every person on taking his seat, as a member, shall pay to the Treasurer an initiation fee of fifty cents. The monthly dues shall be thirty cents, payable in advance.

Sec. 3. In case any officer neglects a duty, he shall, upon motion of a member, and with the consent of the Society, be fined ten cents; and should he still persist in neglecting such duty, he may be removed from his office by a two-third vote of the members present.

Sec. 4. If any member calls another to order and fails to substantiate his point, he shall be fined in accordance with Section first of this Article.

Sec. 5. Any member who shall make use of improper language, or refuse to obey when called to order, shall be fined in accordance with Section first of this Article; and, if he repeat the offense, he may be expelled from the Association by a two-third vote of the members present.

Sec. 6. If any member neglects to pay his fines or dues within two weeks after becoming payable, he shall be notified thereof by the Treasurer, and, if he still neglects payment, he shall, at the next regular meeting after receiving said notice, be suspended for two weeks; and if then in arrears, shall be considered as no longer a member.

Article VI.—Appeals, &c.

Sec. 1. An Appeal may, in all cases, be made from any decision of the President; a two-third vote of the members present shall be necessary to sustain the appeal.

Sec. 2. Any member having made an appeal from

a decision of the President, may sustain such appeal, and the President may give his reasons for his decision, before the question is put, which being passed upon, the matter shall be considered as settled.

Article VII.—Committees.

All Committees shall make their reports in writing.

RULES OF ORDER.

1. The President, or in his absence the Vice President, shall take the Chair at the hour named in Article I., Section 1, of the By-Laws. In the absence of those officers, a President pro tem. shall be chosen by the Society.

2. The President shall be privileged to debate upon all subjects, on calling the Vice President, or any other member willing, to the Chair.

3. After the meeting has been called to order, each member shall take a seat, which he shall be required to occupy during the evening, and shall not interrupt the proceedings by reading or conversation, without permission of the President.

4. No member shall speak on any motion (except the mover thereof) more than twice, nor more than once until all wishing to speak have spoken; neither shall he make or debate an amendment, having spoken twice on the original motion, without permission of the Society.

5. When two or more members rise at the same time, the President shall name the person to speak.

6. When a member shall be called to order by the President or any member, he shall at once take his seat, and every question of order shall be decided by the President without debate.

7. No motion shall be debatable until seconded.

8. Appeals, and motions to reconsider or adjourn, are not debatable.

9. When a question is under debate, no motion shall be received but to lay on the table, to postpone, to commit, or to amend.

10. No member shall interrupt another while speaking, except in accordance with Rule of Order, No. 6.

11. A motion to adjourn shall always be in order, except when another motion is before the Society.

12. When a motion or amendment shall be made and seconded, the mover thereof may be called upon by the President or any member to reduce the same to writing, and hand it in at the table, from which it shall be read before open to the Society for debate.

13. The mover of a motion shall be at liberty to accept any amendment thereto; but if an amendment be offered and not accepted, yet duly seconded, the Association shall pass upon it before voting upon the original motion.

14. Any member may criticise Essays or Recitations delivered before the Society, provided he do not occupy more than five minutes.

15. Before taking the vote on any question, the President shall ask: "Are you ready for the ques-

tion?" Should no one offer to speak, the President shall rise to put the question, and after he has risen, no member shall speak upon it without permission of the Society.

16. When a motion to adjourn is carried, no member shall leave his seat, until the President have left his chair.

17. When a motion has been made and decided, it shall be in order for any member (but such as have voted in the minority), to move the re-consideration thereof, if done within three weeks after being voted upon.

18. Every officer, on leaving his office, shall give to his successor all papers, documents, books and money belonging to the Society.

19. No smoking, and no refreshments, except water, shall be allowed in the Society's rooms.

APPENDIX.

HERE we append, for convenience of reference, and as being what every American should know and understand, a copy (from the Manual prepared for the use of the United States House of Representatives,) of the Constitution of the United States, the Amendments thereto, and several accompanying documents.

CONSTITUTION.

Preamble.

WE, the People of the United States, in order to form a more perfect Union, establish justice, insure domestic tranquillity, provide for the common defense, promote the general welfare, and secure the blessings of liberty to ourselves and our posterity, do ordain and establish this Constitution for the United States of America.

ARTICLE I.

SECTION I.

Congress.

All legislative powers herein granted shall be vested in a Congress of the United

States, which shall consist of a Senate and House of Representatives.

SECTION II.

Representatives, how chosen.

The House of Representatives shall be composed of members chosen every second year by the people of the several States, and the electors in each State shall have the qualifications requisite for electors of the most numerous branch of the State legislature.

Qualification of Representatives.

No person shall be a Representative who shall not have attained the age of twenty-five years, and have been seven years a citizen of the United States, and who shall not, when elected, be an inhabitant of that State in which he shall be chosen.

Apportionment of Representatives, and direct taxes.

Representatives and direct taxes shall be apportioned among the several States which may be included within this Union, according to their respective numbers, which shall be determined by adding to the whole number of free persons, including those bound to service for a term of years, and excluding Indians not taxed, three fifths of all other persons. The actual enumeration shall be made within three years after the first meeting of the Congress of the United States, and within every subsequent term of ten years, in such manner as they shall by law direct. The number of Representatives shall not exceed one for every thirty thousand, but each State shall have at least

Census every ten years.

one representative; and until such enumeration shall be made, the State of *New Hampshire* shall be entitled to choose three, *Massachusetts* eight, *Rhode Island and Providence Plantations* one, *Connecticut* five, *New York* six, *New Jersey* four, *Pennsylvania* eight, *Delaware* one, *Maryland* six, *Virginia* ten, *North Carolina* five, *South Carolina* five, and *Georgia* three.

Vacancies, how filled.

When vacancies happen in the representation from any State, the executive authority thereof shall issue writs of election to fill such vacancies.

Representatives choose officers and bring impeachments.

The House of Representatives shall choose their Speaker and other officers; and shall have the sole power of impeachment.

SECTION III.

Senate, how chosen.

The Senate of the United States shall be composed of two Senators from each State, chosen by the legislature thereof, for six years; and each Senator shall have one vote.

Senators classed.

Immediately after they shall be assembled in consequence of the first election, they shall be divided as equally as may be into three classes. The seats of the Senators of the first class shall be vacated at the expiration of the second year; of the second class, at the expiration of the fourth year; and of the third class, at the expiration of the sixth year; so that one third may be chosen every second year: and if vacancies happen by resignation or otherwise during the recess of the legislature of any State, the executive thereof may make temporary appointments until the next meeting of the legislature, which shall then fill such vacancies.

Vacancies, how filled.

Qualifications of Senators.

No person shall be a Senator who shall not have attained to the age of thirty years, and been nine years a citizen of the United States, and who shall not, when elected, be an inhabitant of that State for which he shall be chosen.

Vice President to preside.

The Vice President of the United States shall be President of the Senate, but shall have no vote unless they be equally divided.

Officers of Senate.

The Senate shall choose their other officers, and also a President *pro tempore* in the absence of the Vice President, or when he shall exercise the office of President of the United States.

Trial of impeachments.

The Senate shall have the sole power to try all impeachments. When sitting for that purpose, they shall be on oath or affirmation. When the President of the United States is tried, the Chief Justice shall preside: and no person shall be convicted without the concurrence of two thirds of the members present.

Judgment in impeachments.

Judgment in cases of impeachment shall not extend further than to removal from office and disqualification to hold and enjoy any office of honor, trust, or profit under the United States; but the party convicted shall nevertheless be liable and subject to indictment, trial, judgment, and punishment, according to law. **Effect of.**

SECTION IV.

The times, places, and manner of holding elections for Senators and Representatives shall be prescribed in each State by the legislature thereof; but the Congress may at any time, by law, make or alter such regulations, except as to the places of choosing Senators. **Elections, when and how held.**

The Congress shall assemble at least once in every year, and such meeting shall be on the first Monday in December, unless they shall by law appoint a different day. **Congress assemble annually.**

SECTION V.

Each house shall be the judge of the elections, returns and qualifications of its own members, and a majority of each shall constitute a quorum to do business; but a smaller number may adjourn from day to day, and may be authorized to compel the attendance of absent members, in such manner, and under such penalties, as each house may provide. **Elections, how judged.** **Quorum.** **Absent members.**

Each house may determine the rules of its proceedings, punish its members for **Rules.**

Expulsion.

disorderly behavior, and with the concurrence of two thirds, expel a member.

Journals to be kept and published.

Each house shall keep a journal of its proceedings, and from time to time publish the same, excepting such parts as may in their judgment require secresy; and the yeas and nays of the members of either house on any question shall, at the desire of one fifth of those present, be entered on the journal.

Yeas and nays.

Adjournments.

Neither house, during the session of Congress, shall, without the consent of the other, adjourn for more than three days, nor to any other place than that in which the two houses shall be sitting.

SECTION VI.

Compensation.

The Senators and Representatives shall receive a compensation for their services, to be ascertained by law, and paid out of the Treasury of the United States. They shall in all cases, except treason, felony, and breach of the peace, be privileged from arrest during their attendance at the session of their respective houses, and in going to and returning from the same; and for any speech or debate in either house, they shall not be questioned in any other place.

Privilege.

Members not appointed to office.

No Senator or Representative shall, during the time for which he was elected, be appointed to any civil office under the authority of the United States which shall have been created, or the emoluments whereof shall have been increased, during such time; and no person holding any office under the United States, shall be a member of either house during his continuance in office. **Officers of government can not be members.**

SECTION VII.

All bills for raising revenue shall originate in the House of Representatives; but the Senate may propose or concur with amendments as on other bills. **Revenue bills.**

Every bill which shall have passed the House of Representatives and the Senate, shall, before it become a law, be presented to the President of the United States; if he approve he shall sign it; but if not, he shall return it, with his objections, to that house in which it shall have originated, who shall enter the objections at large on their journal, and proceed to reconsider it. If after such reconsideration two-thirds of that house shall agree to pass the bill, it shall be sent, together with the objections, to the other house, by which it shall likewise be reconsidered, and if approved by two-thirds of that house, it shall become a law. But in all such cases the votes of both houses shall be determined by yeas and nays, and the names of the persons voting for and against the bill shall be entered on **Bills to be presented to the President.** **His powers over them.** **Proceedings on his veto.**

Bills to be laws if not returned in ten days.

the journal of each house respectively. If any bill shall not be returned by the President within ten days (Sundays excepted) after it shall have been presented to him, the same shall be a law, in like manner as if he had signed it, unless the Congress by their adjournment prevent its return, in which case it shall not be a law.

Joint orders or resolutions to be approved by the President.

Every order, resolution, or vote, to which the concurrence of the Senate and House of Representatives may be necessary, (except on a question of adjournment,) shall be presented to the President of the United States; and before the same shall take effect, shall be approved by him, or, being disapproved by him, shall be repassed by two-thirds of the Senate and House of Representatives, according to the rules and limitations prescribed in the case of a bill.

SECTION VIII.

Powers of Congress to lay taxes—pay debts.

General welfare.

Duties uniform.

The Congress shall have power to lay and collect taxes, duties, imposts and excises, to pay the debts and provide for the common defense and general welfare of the United States; but all duties, imposts and excises, shall be uniform throughout the United States;

Borrow money.

To borrow money on the credit of the United States;

To regulate commerce with foreign nations, and among the several States, and with the Indian tribes; Commerce.

To establish a uniform rule of naturalization, and uniform laws on the subject of bankruptcies throughout the United States; Naturalization. Bankruptcy.

To coin money, regulate the value thereof, and of foreign coin, and fix the standard of weights and measures; Coin money. Weights and measures.

To provide for the punishment of counterfeiting the securities and current coin of the United States; Counterfeiting.

To establish post offices and post roads; Post roads.

To promote the progress of science and useful arts, by securing, for limited times, to authors and inventors the exclusive right to their respective writings and discoveries; Promote arts and science.

To constitute tribunals inferior to the Supreme Court; Inferior courts.

To define and punish piracies and felonies committed on the high seas, and offenses against the law of nations; Piracies, &c.

To declare war, grant letters of marque and reprisal, and make rules concerning captures on land and water; Declare war and make captures.

To raise and support armies; but no appropriation of money to that use shall be for a longer term than two years; Raise armies.

To provide and maintain a navy; Navy.

Rules and articles of war.

To make rules for the government and regulation of the land and naval forces;

Call out militia.

To provide for calling forth the militia to execute the laws of the Union, suppress insurrections, and repel invasions;

Organize and govern militia.

Officers of militia.

To provide for organizing, arming and disciplining the militia, and for governing such part of them as may be employed in the service of the United States, reserving to the States, respectively, the appointment of the officers, and the authority of training the militia according to the discipline prescribed by Congress;

Exclusive legislation over seat of government.

And over forts, arsenals, docks, &c.

To exercise exclusive legislation in all cases whatsoever, over such district (not exceeding ten miles square) as may by cession of particular States, and the acceptance of Congress, become the seat of the government of the United States, and to exercise like authority over all places purchased by the consent of the legislature of the State in which the same shall be, for the erection of forts, magazines, arsenals, dock-yards, and other needful buildings; and

To make general laws to carry powers into effect.

To make all laws which shall be necessary and proper for carrying into execution the foregoing powers, and all other powers vested by this Constitution in the Government of the United States, or in any department or officer thereof.

SECTION IX.

The migration or importation of such persons as any of the States now existing shall think proper to admit, shall not be prohibited by the Congress prior to the year one thousand eight hundred and eight; but a tax or duty may be imposed on such importation, not exceeding ten dollars for each person. **Importation of slaves allowed till 1808.**

The privilege of the writ of habeas corpus shall not be suspended, unless when in cases of rebellion or invasion the public safety may require it. **Habeas corpus.**

No bill of attainder or *ex post facto* law shall be passed. **Attainder and ex post facto laws.**

No capitation or other direct tax shall be laid unless in proportion to the census or enumeration herein before directed to be taken. **Direct taxes.**

No tax or duty shall be laid on articles exported from any State. **No exportation duty.**

No preference shall be given by any regulation of commerce or revenue to the ports of one State over those of another; nor shall vessels bound to or from one State, be obliged to enter, clear, or pay duties in another. **Commerce between the States.**

No money shall be drawn from the treasury, but in consequence of appropriations made by law; and a regular statement and account of the receipts and ex- **Money, how drawn from the treasury.**

To be published. penditures of all public money shall be published from time to time.

No nobility. No title of nobility shall be granted by the United States: and no person holding any office of profit or trust under them, shall, without the consent of the Congress, accept of any present, emolument, office or title, of any kind whatever, from any king, prince, or foreign state.

Foreign presents and titles.

SECTION X.

Powers denied to the States.

No State shall enter into any treaty, alliance, or confederation; grant letters of marque and reprisal; coin money; emit bills of credit; make any thing but gold and silver coin a tender in payment of debts; pass any bill of attainder, ex post facto law, or law impairing the obligation of contracts, or grant any title of nobility.

Other powers denied to States.

No State shall, without the consent of the Congress, lay any imposts or duties on imports or exports, except what may be absolutely necessary for executing its inspection laws; and the net produce of all duties and imposts, laid by any State on imports or exports, shall be for the use of the Treasury of the United States; and all such laws shall be subject to the revision and control of the Congress.

Further denial of powers to States.

No State shall, without the consent of Congress, lay any duty of tonnage, keep troops or ships of war in time of peace, enter into any agreement or compact with another State, or with a foreign power, or engage in war, unless actually invaded, or in such imminent danger as will not admit of delay.

ARTICLE II.

SECTION I.

The Executive power shall be vested in a President of the United States of America. He shall hold his office during the term of four years, and together with the Vice President, chosen for the same term, be elected as follows: **President of the United States.**

Each State shall appoint, in such manner as the legislature thereof may direct, a number of electors, equal to the whole number of Senators and Representatives to which the State may be entitled in the Congress; but no Senator or Representative, or person holding an office of trust or profit under the United States, shall be appointed an elector. **Electors, how appointed.**

The electors shall meet in their respective States, and vote by ballot for two persons, of whom one at least shall not be an inhabitant of the same State with themselves. And they shall make a list of all the persons voted for, and of the number of votes for each; which list they shall sign and certify, and transmit sealed to the seat of the government of the United **Electors to meet and to elect a President and Vice President.**

States, directed to the President of the Senate. The President of the Senate shall, in the presence of the Senate and House of Representatives, open all the certificates, and the votes shall then be counted. The person having the greatest number of votes shall be the President, if such number be a majority of the whole number of electors appointed; and if there be more than one who have such majority, and have an equal number of votes, then the House of Representatives shall immediately choose, by ballot, one of them for President; and if no person have a majority, then from the five highest on the list the said House shall in like manner choose the President. But in choosing the President, the votes shall be taken by States, the representation from each State having one vote; a quorum for this purpose shall consist of a member or members from two-thirds of the States, and a majority of all the States shall be necessary to a choice. In every case, after the choice of a President, the person having the greatest number of votes of the electors shall be the Vice President. But if there should remain two or more who have equal votes, the Senate shall choose from them by ballot the Vice President.*

Their votes counted in Congress.

Representatives to choose, if electors fail.

Votes by States.

Vice President.

* This clause of the Constitution has been amended. See twelfth article of the amendments, page 296.

The Congress may determine the time of choosing the electors, and the day on which they shall give their votes; which day shall be the same throughout the United States. **Election and meeting of electors.**

No person except a natural-born citizen, or a citizen of the United States at the time of the adoption of this Constitution, shall be eligible to the office of President; neither shall any person be eligible to that office who shall not have attained to the age of thirty-five years, and been fourteen years a resident within the United States. **Qualification of President.**

In case of the removal of the President from office, or of his death, resignation, or inability to discharge the powers and duties of the said office, the same shall devolve on the Vice President, and the Congress may by law provide for the case of removal, death, resignation, or inability, both of the President and Vice President, declaring what officer shall act as President, and such officer shall act accordingly, until the disability be removed or a President shall be elected. **Removal, death, &c., of President.**

The President shall, at stated times, receive for his services a compensation which shall neither be increased nor diminished during the period for which he shall have been elected, and he shall not receive within that period any other **Compensation of President.**

emolument from the United States, or any of them.

Before he enter on the execution of his office, he shall take the following oath or affirmation:

Oath.

"I do solemnly swear (or affirm) that I will faithfully execute the office of President of the United States; and will, to the best of my ability, preserve, protect, and defend the Constitution of the United States."

SECTION II.

Powers and duties of the President.

The President shall be commander-in-chief of the army and navy of the United States, and of the militia of the several States when called into the actual service of the United States; he may require the opinion, in writing, of the principal officer in each of the executive departments, upon any subject relating to the duties of their respective offices; and he shall have power to grant reprieves and pardons for offenses against the United States, except in cases of impeachment.

He shall have power, by and with the advice and consent of the Senate, to make treaties, provided two-thirds of the Senators present concur; and he shall nominate, and, by and with the advice and consent of the Senate, shall appoint ambassadors, other public ministers and con-

Appointment of public officers.

suls, judges of the Supreme Court, and all other officers of the United States whose appointments are not herein otherwise provided for, and which shall be established by law; but the Congress may by law vest the appointment of such inferior officers as they think proper, in the President alone, in the courts of law, or in the heads of departments.

Vacancies in office.

The President shall have power to fill up all vacancies that may happen during the recess of the Senate, by granting commissions which shall expire at the end of their next session.

SECTION III.

Further powers and duties of the President.

He shall from time to time give to the Congress information of the state of the Union, and recommend to their consideration such measures as he shall judge necessary and expedient; he may, on extraordinary occasions, convene both houses, or either of them, and in case of disagreement between them with respect to the time of adjournment, he may adjourn them to such time as he shall think proper; he shall receive ambassadors and other public ministers; he shall take care that the laws be faithfully executed, and shall commission all the officers of the United States.

SECTION IV.

Impeachment.

The President, Vice President, and all civil officers of the United States, shall be removed from office on impeachment for and conviction of treason, bribery, or other high crimes and misdemeanors.

ARTICLE III.

SECTION I.

Judiciary and tenure of judges.

The judicial power of the United States shall be vested in one Supreme Court, and in such inferior courts as the Congress may from time to time ordain and establish. The judges, both of the supreme and inferior courts, shall hold their offices during good behavior, and shall, at stated times, receive for their services a compensation, which shall not be diminished during their continuance in office.

SECTION II.

Powers of the judiciary.

The judicial power shall extend to all cases, in law and equity, arising under this Constitution, the laws of the United States, and treaties made, or which shall be made, under their authority; to all cases affecting ambassadors, other public ministers and consuls; to all cases of admiralty and maritime jurisdiction; to controversies to which the United States shall be a party; to controversies between two or more States; between a State and citizens of another

State; between citizens of different States; between citizens of the same State claiming lands under grants of different States; and between a State, or the citizens thereof, and foreign States, citizens, or subjects.

Jurisdiction of the Supreme Court. In all cases affecting ambassadors, other public ministers, and consuls, and those in which a State shall be a party, the Supreme Court shall have original jurisdiction. In all the other cases before mentioned, the Supreme Court shall have appellate jurisdiction, both as to law and fact, with such exceptions and under such regulations as the Congress shall make.

Trials by jury. The trial of all crimes, except in cases of impeachment, shall be by jury; and **And where held.** such trial shall be held in the State where the said crimes shall have been committed; but when not committed within any State, the trial shall be at such place or places as the Congress may by law have directed.

SECTION III.

Treason. Treason against the United States shall consist only in levying war against them, or in adhering to their enemies, giving them aid and comfort. No person shall be convicted of treason unless on the testimony of two witnesses to the same overt act, or on confession in open court.

The Congress shall have power to declare the punishment of treason; but no

No corruption of blood.

attainder of treason shall work corruption of blood or forfeiture, except during the life of the person attainted.

ARTICLE IV.

SECTION I.

Acts of States accredited.

Full faith and credit shall be given in each State to the public acts, records, and judicial proceeding of every other State. And the Congress may, by general laws, prescribe the manner in which such acts, records, and proceedings shall be proved, and the effect thereof.

SECTION II.

Privileges of citizenship.

The citizens of each State shall be entitled to all privileges and immunities of citizens in the several States.

Fugitives from justice to be delivered up.

A person charged in any State with treason, felony, or other crime, who shall flee from justice, and be found in another State, shall, on demand of the Executive authority of the State from which he fled, be delivered up, to be removed to the State having jurisdiction of the crime.

Fugitive slaves to be delivered up.

No person held to service or labor in one State, under the laws thereof, escaping into another, shall, in consequence of any law or regulation therein, be discharged from such service or labor, but shall be delivered up on claim of the party to whom such service or labor may be due.

SECTION III.

New States may be admitted by the Congress into this Union; but no new State shall be formed or erected within the jurisdiction of any other State; nor any State be formed by the junction of two or more States, or parts of States, without the consent of the legislatures of the States concerned, as well as of the Congress. **New States.**

The Congress shall have power to dispose of and make all needful rules and regulations respecting the territory or other property belonging to the United States; and nothing in this Constitution shall be so construed as to prejudice any claims of the United States, or of any particular State. **Territory and other property of the United States.**

SECTION IV.

The United States shall guaranty to every State in this Union a republican form of government, and shall protect each of them against invasion, and, on application of the legislature, or of the Executive (when the legislature can not be convened), against domestic violence. **Republican form of government.** **Protection of States.**

ARTICLE V.

Amendments of this Constitution.

The Congress, whenever two-thirds of both houses shall deem it necessary, shall propose amendments to this Constitution, or, on the application of the legislatures of two-thirds of the several States, shall call a convention for proposing amendments, which, in either case, shall be valid to all intents and purposes, as part of this Constitution, when ratified by the legislatures of three-fourths of the several States, or by conventions in three-fourths thereof, as the one or the other mode of ratification may be proposed by the Congress; provided that no amendment which may be made prior to the year one thousand eight hundred and eight, shall in any manner affect the first and fourth clauses in the ninth section of the first article; and that no State, without its consent, shall be deprived of its equal suffrage in the Senate.

ARTICLE VI.

Debts of former government recognized.

All debts contracted and engagements entered into before the adoption of this Constitution, shall be as valid against the United States under this Constitution, as under the confederation.

This Constitution, and the laws of the United States which shall be made in pursuance thereof, and all treaties made, or which shall be made, under the authority of the United States, shall be the supreme law of the land; and the judges in every State shall be bound thereby, any thing in the Constitution or laws of any State to the contrary notwithstanding.

What constitutes the supreme law.

The Senators and Representatives before mentioned, and the members of the several State legislatures, and all executive and judicial officers, both of the United States and of the several States, shall be bound by oath or affirmation to support this Constitution; but no religious test shall ever be required as a qualification to any office or public trust under the United States.

Oath of public officers.

No religious test.

ARTICLE VII.

The ratification of the conventions of nine States, shall be sufficient for the establishment of this Constitution between the States so ratifying the same.

Ratification.

Done in convention, by the unanimous consent of the States present, the seventeenth day of September, in the year of our Lord one thousand seven hundred and eighty-seven, and of the Independence of the United States of America the twelfth. In witness whereof, we have hereunto subscribed our names.

GEO: WASHINGTON,

President, and Deputy from Virginia.

NEW HAMPSHIRE.

John Langdon,
Nicholas Gilman.

MASSACHUSETTS.

Nathaniel Gorham,
Rufus King.

CONNECTICUT.

William Samuel Johnson,
Roger Sherman.

NEW YORK.

Alexander Hamilton.

NEW JERSEY.

William Livingston,
David Brearley,
William Paterson,
Jonathan Dayton.

PENNSYLVANIA.

B. Franklin,
Thomas Mifflin,
Robert Morris,
George Clymer,
Thomas Fitzsimons,
Jared Ingersoll,
James Wilson,
Gouv. Morris.

DELAWARE.

George Read,
Gunning Bedford, jun.,
John Dickinson,
Richard Bassett,
Jacob Broom.

MARYLAND.

James McHenry,
Dan of St. Thomas Jenifer,
Daniel Carroll.

VIRGINIA.

John Blair,
James Madison, jun.

NORTH CAROLINA.

William Blount,
Rich'd Dobbs Spaight,
Hu. Williamson.

SOUTH CAROLINA.

J. Rutledge,
Charles Cotesworth Pinckney,
Charles Pinckney,
Pierce Butler.

GEORGIA.

William Few,
Abr. Baldwin.

Attest: WILLIAM JACKSON, *Secretary.*

PROCEEDINGS

OF THE

CONVENTION WHICH FORMED THE CONSTITUTION

IN CONVENTION.

MONDAY, *September* 17, 1787.

Resolved, That the preceding Constitution be laid before the United States in Congress assembled; and that it is the opinion of this Convention that it should afterward be submitted to a convention of delegates, chosen in each State by the people thereof, under the recommendation of its legislature, for their assent and ratification; and that each convention assenting to and ratifying the same should give notice thereof to the United States in Congress assembled.

Resolved, That it is the opinion of this Convention that, as soon as the conventions of nine States shall have ratified this Constitution, the United States in Congress assembled should fix a day on which electors should be appointed by the States which shall have ratified the same, and a day on which electors should assemble to vote for the President, and the time and place for commencing proceedings under this Constitution; that after such publication, the electors should be appointed, and the Senators and Representatives elected; that the electors should meet on the day fixed for the election of the President, and should transmit their votes, certified, signed, sealed, and directed, as the Constitution requires, to the Secretary of the United States in Congress assembled; that the Senators and Representatives should convene at the time and place assigned; that the Senators should appoint a President of the Senate, for the sole purpose of receiving, opening, and counting the votes for President; and that, after he shall be chosen, the Congress, together with the President, should, without delay, proceed to execute this Constitution.

By the unanimous order of the Convention:

GEO: WASHINGTON, *President.*

WILLIAM JACKSON, *Secretary.*

LETTER OF THE CONVENTION TO THE OLD CONGRESS.

IN CONVENTION.

SEPTEMBER 17, 1787.

SIR: We have now the honor to submit to the consideration of the United States in Congress assembled, that Constitution which has appeared to us the most advisable.

The friends of our country have long seen and desired that the power of making war, peace, and treaties; that of levying money, and regulating commerce, and the correspondent executive and judicial authorities, should be fully and effectually vested in the General Government of the Union: but the impropriety of delegating such extensive trust to one body of men is evident; hence results the necessity of a different organization.

It is obviously impracticable in the federal government of these States to secure all rights of independent sovereignty to each, and yet provide for the interest and safety of all. Individuals entering into society must give up a share of liberty to preserve the rest. The magnitude of the sacrifice must depend as well on situation and circumstance as on the object to be obtained. It is at all times difficult to draw with precision the line between those rights which must be surrendered and those which may be reserved; and, on the present occasion, this difficulty was increased by a difference among the several States as to their situation, extent, habits, and particular interests.

In all our deliberations on this subject, we kept steadily in our view that which appears to us the greatest interest of every true American—the consolidation of our Union—in which is involved our prosperity, felicity, safety, perhaps our national existence. This important consideration, seriously and deeply impressed on our minds, led each State in the Convention to be less rigid on points of inferior magnitude than might have been otherwise expected; and thus the Constitution which we now present is the result of a spirit of amity, and of that mutual deference and concession which the peculiarity of our political situation rendered indispensable.

That it will meet the full and entire approbation of every State, is not, perhaps, to be expected; but each will doubtless consider that, had her interest been alone consulted, the consequences might have been particularly disagreeable or injurious to others. That it is liable to as few exceptions as could reasonably have been expected, we hope and believe. That it may promote the lasting welfare of that country so dear to us all, and secure her freedom and happiness, is our most ardent wish.

With great respect, we have the honor to be, Sir, your Excellency's most obedient, humble servants.

By unanimous order of the Convention:

GEO: WASHINGTON, *President.*

His Excellency the PRESIDENT OF CONGRESS.

PROCEEDINGS IN THE OLD CONGRESS.

UNITED STATES IN CONGRESS ASSEMBLED.

FRIDAY, *September* 28, 1787

Present.—New Hampshire, Massachusetts, Connecticut, New York, New Jersey, Pennsylvania, Delaware, Virginia, North Carolina, South Carolina, and Georgia; and from Maryland, Mr. Ross.

Congress having received the report of the Convention lately assembled in Philadelphia—

Resolved, unanimously, That the said report, with

the resolutions and letter accompanying the same, be transmitted to the several legislatures, in order to be submitted to a convention of delegates chosen in each State by the people thereof, in conformity to the resolves in the Convention made and provided in that case.

CHARLES THOMSON, *Secretary.*

AMENDMENTS.

ARTICLE I.

Congress shall make no law respecting an establishment of religion, or prohibiting the free exercise thereof; or abridging the freedom of speech, or of the press; or the right of the people peaceably to assemble, and to petition the government for a redress of grievances.

ARTICLE II.

A well regulated militia being necessary to the security of a free State, the right of the people to keep and bear arms shall not be infringed.

ARTICLE III.

No soldier shall, in time of peace, be quartered in any house without the consent of the owner, nor in time of war but in a manner to be prescribed by law.

ARTICLE IV.

The right of the people to be secure in their persons, houses, papers, and effects, against unreasonable searches and seizures, shall not be violated, and no warrants shall issue but upon probable cause, supported by oath or affirmation, and particularly describing the place to be searched, and the persons or things to be seized.

ARTICLE V.

No person shall be held to answer for a capital, or otherwise infamous crime, unless on a presentment or indictment of a grand jury, except in cases arising in the land or naval forces, or in the militia, when in actual service in time of war or public danger; nor shall any person be subject for the same offense to be twice put in jeopardy of life or limb; nor shall be compelled in any criminal case to be a witness against himself, nor be deprived of life, liberty, or property, without due process of law; nor shall private property be taken for public use without just compensation.

ARTICLE VI.

In all criminal prosecutions, the accused shall enjoy the right to a speedy and public trial by an impartial jury of the State and district wherein the crime shall have been committed, which district shall have been previously ascertained by law, and to be informed of the nature and cause of the accusation; to be confronted with the witnesses against him; to have compulsory process for obtaining witnesses in his favor, and to have the assistance of counsel for his defense.

ARTICLE VII.

In suits at common law, where the value in controversy shall exceed twenty dollars, the right of trial by jury shall be preserved, and no fact tried by a jury shall be otherwise reëxamined in any court of the United States, than according to the rules of the common law.

ARTICLE VIII.

Excessive bail shall not be required, nor excessive fines imposed, nor cruel and unusual punishments inflicted.

ARTICLE IX.

The enumeration in the Constitution of certain rights, shall not be construed to deny or disparage others retained by the people.

ARTICLE X.

The powers not delegated to the United States by the Constitution, nor prohibited by it to the States, are reserved to the States respectively, or to the people.

ARTICLE XI.

The judicial power of the United States shall not be construed to extend to any suit in law or equity, commenced or prosecuted against one of the United States by citizens of another State, or by citizens or subjects of any foreign State.

ARTICLE XII.

The electors shall meet in their respective States, and vote by ballot for President and Vice President, one of whom at least shall not be an inhabitant of the same State with themselves; they shall name in their ballots the person voted for as President, and in distinct ballots the person voted for as Vice President; and they shall make distinct lists of all persons voted for as President, and of all persons voted for as Vice President, and of the number of votes for each; which lists they shall sign and certify, and transmit sealed to the seat of the government of the United States, directed to the President of the Senate. The President of the Senate shall, in the presence of the Senate and House of Representatives, open all the certificates, and the votes shall then be counted; the person having the greatest number of votes for President shall be the President, if such number be a majority of the whole number of electors appointed; and if no person have such majority, then from the persons having the highest numbers, not exceeding three, on the list of those voted for as President, the House of Representatives shall choose immediately by ballot the President. But in choosing the President, the votes shall be taken by States, the representation from each State having one vote; a quorum for this purpose shall consist of a member or members from two-thirds of the States, and a majority of all the States shall be necessary to a choice. And if the House of Representatives shall not choose a President, whenever the right of choice shall devolve upon them, before the fourth day of March next following, then the Vice President shall act as President, as in the case of the death, or other constitutional disability of the President.

The person having the greatest number of votes as Vice President shall be the Vice President, if such number be a majority of the whole number of electors appointed; and if no person have a majority, then from the two highest numbers on the list the Senate shall choose the Vice President; a quorum for the purpose shall consist of two-thirds of the whole number of Senators, and a majority of the whole number shall be necessary to a choice. But no person constitutionally ineligible to the office of President shall be eligible to that of Vice President of the United States.

INDEX

TO

THE CONSTITUTION OF THE UNITED STATES.

A.

B.

D.

E.

Q.

R.

THE END.

www.ingramcontent.com/pod-product-compliance
Lightning Source LLC
LaVergne TN
LVHW020230110826
845151LV00003B/877

* 9 7 8 1 4 2 5 5 3 1 5 0 8 *